The Gender Dysphoria Journal
© 2022 by Emma Roberts

All rights reserved. No part of this publication may be reproduced, distributed, or transmitted in any form or by any means, including photocopying, recording, or other electronic or mechanical methods, without the prior written permission of the publisher, except in the case of brief quotations embodied in critical reviews and certain other noncommercial uses permitted by copyright law.

Printed in the United States of America
First Printing, 2022.
ISBN 978-1-938249-20-4 (paperback)

Cover design by BookCoverZone.com

Date:_____ Time:_____

Is the feeling good or bad?

How strong is the feeling? (Circle a number)

1   2   3   4   5   6   7   8   9   10

How would you categorize this feeling?
- Difference between the gender I feel I am and the sex I was assigned at birth
- Wanting to remove or change my body parts
- Wanting to have the body parts of another gender
- Wanting to be a different gender than the sex assigned at birth
- Wanting to be treated as a different gender
- Feeling or reacting that is typical for a different gender

Did the feeling have a negative impact? If so, how did it impact you?
- On my emotional health
- On my friends, family, or social life
- On my work or education
- On my self-care (diet, sleep, hygiene, exercise)
- No negative impact

Write out your thoughts:

Date:_____ **Time:**_____

Is the feeling good or bad?

How strong is the feeling? (Circle a number)

1   2   3   4   5   6   7   8   9   10

How would you categorize this feeling?
- Difference between the gender I feel I am and the sex I was assigned at birth
- Wanting to remove or change my body parts
- Wanting to have the body parts of another gender
- Wanting to be a different gender than the sex assigned at birth
- Wanting to be treated as a different gender
- Feeling or reacting that is typical for a different gender

Did the feeling have a negative impact? If so, how did it impact you?
- On my emotional health
- On my friends, family, or social life
- On my work or education
- On my self-care (diet, sleep, hygiene, exercise)
- No negative impact

Write out your thoughts:

Date:_____ Time:_____

Is the feeling good or bad?

How strong is the feeling? (Circle a number)

1 2 3 4 5 6 7 8 9 10

How would you categorize this feeling?
- Difference between the gender I feel I am and the sex I was assigned at birth
- Wanting to remove or change my body parts
- Wanting to have the body parts of another gender
- Wanting to be a different gender than the sex assigned at birth
- Wanting to be treated as a different gender
- Feeling or reacting that is typical for a different gender

Did the feeling have a negative impact? If so, how did it impact you?
- On my emotional health
- On my friends, family, or social life
- On my work or education
- On my self-care (diet, sleep, hygiene, exercise)
- No negative impact

Write out your thoughts:

Date:_____ Time:_____

Is the feeling good or bad?

How strong is the feeling? (Circle a number)

1 2 3 4 5 6 7 8 9 10

How would you categorize this feeling?
- ○ Difference between the gender I feel I am and the sex I was assigned at birth
- ○ Wanting to remove or change my body parts
- ○ Wanting to have the body parts of another gender
- ○ Wanting to be a different gender than the sex assigned at birth
- ○ Wanting to be treated as a different gender
- ○ Feeling or reacting that is typical for a different gender

Did the feeling have a negative impact? If so, how did it impact you?
- ○ On my emotional health
- ○ On my friends, family, or social life
- ○ On my work or education
- ○ On my self-care (diet, sleep, hygiene, exercise)
- ○ No negative impact

Write out your thoughts:

Date:_____ Time:_____

Is the feeling good or bad?

How strong is the feeling? (Circle a number)

1   2   3   4   5   6   7   8   9   10

How would you categorize this feeling?

- ○ Difference between the gender I feel I am and the sex I was assigned at birth
- ○ Wanting to remove or change my body parts
- ○ Wanting to have the body parts of another gender
- ○ Wanting to be a different gender than the sex assigned at birth
- ○ Wanting to be treated as a different gender
- ○ Feeling or reacting that is typical for a different gender

Did the feeling have a negative impact? If so, how did it impact you?

- ○ On my emotional health
- ○ On my friends, family, or social life
- ○ On my work or education
- ○ On my self-care (diet, sleep, hygiene, exercise)
- ○ No negative impact

Write out your thoughts:

Date:_____ Time:_____

Is the feeling good or bad?

How strong is the feeling? (Circle a number)

1   2   3   4   5   6   7   8   9   10

How would you categorize this feeling?
- Difference between the gender I feel I am and the sex I was assigned at birth
- Wanting to remove or change my body parts
- Wanting to have the body parts of another gender
- Wanting to be a different gender than the sex assigned at birth
- Wanting to be treated as a different gender
- Feeling or reacting that is typical for a different gender

Did the feeling have a negative impact? If so, how did it impact you?
- On my emotional health
- On my friends, family, or social life
- On my work or education
- On my self-care (diet, sleep, hygiene, exercise)
- No negative impact

Write out your thoughts:

Date:_____ Time:_____

Is the feeling good or bad?

How strong is the feeling? (Circle a number)
1   2   3   4   5   6   7   8   9   10

How would you categorize this feeling?
- ○ Difference between the gender I feel I am and the sex I was assigned at birth
- ○ Wanting to remove or change my body parts
- ○ Wanting to have the body parts of another gender
- ○ Wanting to be a different gender than the sex assigned at birth
- ○ Wanting to be treated as a different gender
- ○ Feeling or reacting that is typical for a different gender

Did the feeling have a negative impact? If so, how did it impact you?
- ○ On my emotional health
- ○ On my friends, family, or social life
- ○ On my work or education
- ○ On my self-care (diet, sleep, hygiene, exercise)
- ○ No negative impact

Write out your thoughts:

Date:_____ Time:_____

Is the feeling good or bad?

How strong is the feeling? (Circle a number)

1 2 3 4 5 6 7 8 9 10

How would you categorize this feeling?
- Difference between the gender I feel I am and the sex I was assigned at birth
- Wanting to remove or change my body parts
- Wanting to have the body parts of another gender
- Wanting to be a different gender than the sex assigned at birth
- Wanting to be treated as a different gender
- Feeling or reacting that is typical for a different gender

Did the feeling have a negative impact? If so, how did it impact you?
- On my emotional health
- On my friends, family, or social life
- On my work or education
- On my self-care (diet, sleep, hygiene, exercise)
- No negative impact

Write out your thoughts:

Date:_____ Time:_____

Is the feeling good or bad?

How strong is the feeling? (Circle a number)

1   2   3   4   5   6   7   8   9   10

How would you categorize this feeling?
- Difference between the gender I feel I am and the sex I was assigned at birth
- Wanting to remove or change my body parts
- Wanting to have the body parts of another gender
- Wanting to be a different gender than the sex assigned at birth
- Wanting to be treated as a different gender
- Feeling or reacting that is typical for a different gender

Did the feeling have a negative impact? If so, how did it impact you?
- On my emotional health
- On my friends, family, or social life
- On my work or education
- On my self-care (diet, sleep, hygiene, exercise)
- No negative impact

Write out your thoughts:

Date:_____ Time:_____

Is the feeling good or bad?

How strong is the feeling? (Circle a number)

1   2   3   4   5   6   7   8   9   10

How would you categorize this feeling?
- Difference between the gender I feel I am and the sex I was assigned at birth
- Wanting to remove or change my body parts
- Wanting to have the body parts of another gender
- Wanting to be a different gender than the sex assigned at birth
- Wanting to be treated as a different gender
- Feeling or reacting that is typical for a different gender

Did the feeling have a negative impact? If so, how did it impact you?
- On my emotional health
- On my friends, family, or social life
- On my work or education
- On my self-care (diet, sleep, hygiene, exercise)
- No negative impact

Write out your thoughts:

Date:_____ **Time:**_____

Is the feeling good or bad?

How strong is the feeling? (Circle a number)

1   2   3   4   5   6   7   8   9   10

How would you categorize this feeling?
- Difference between the gender I feel I am and the sex I was assigned at birth
- Wanting to remove or change my body parts
- Wanting to have the body parts of another gender
- Wanting to be a different gender than the sex assigned at birth
- Wanting to be treated as a different gender
- Feeling or reacting that is typical for a different gender

Did the feeling have a negative impact? If so, how did it impact you?
- On my emotional health
- On my friends, family, or social life
- On my work or education
- On my self-care (diet, sleep, hygiene, exercise)
- No negative impact

Write out your thoughts:

Date:_____ Time:_____

Is the feeling good or bad?

How strong is the feeling? (Circle a number)

1 2 3 4 5 6 7 8 9 10

How would you categorize this feeling?

- ○ Difference between the gender I feel I am and the sex I was assigned at birth
- ○ Wanting to remove or change my body parts
- ○ Wanting to have the body parts of another gender
- ○ Wanting to be a different gender than the sex assigned at birth
- ○ Wanting to be treated as a different gender
- ○ Feeling or reacting that is typical for a different gender

Did the feeling have a negative impact? If so, how did it impact you?

- ○ On my emotional health
- ○ On my friends, family, or social life
- ○ On my work or education
- ○ On my self-care (diet, sleep, hygiene, exercise)
- ○ No negative impact

Write out your thoughts:

Date:_____ Time:_____

Is the feeling good or bad?

How strong is the feeling? (Circle a number)

1   2   3   4   5   6   7   8   9   10

How would you categorize this feeling?
- Difference between the gender I feel I am and the sex I was assigned at birth
- Wanting to remove or change my body parts
- Wanting to have the body parts of another gender
- Wanting to be a different gender than the sex assigned at birth
- Wanting to be treated as a different gender
- Feeling or reacting that is typical for a different gender

Did the feeling have a negative impact? If so, how did it impact you?
- On my emotional health
- On my friends, family, or social life
- On my work or education
- On my self-care (diet, sleep, hygiene, exercise)
- No negative impact

Write out your thoughts:

Date:_____ **Time:**_____

Is the feeling good or bad?

How strong is the feeling? (Circle a number)

1   2   3   4   5   6   7   8   9   10

How would you categorize this feeling?
- Difference between the gender I feel I am and the sex I was assigned at birth
- Wanting to remove or change my body parts
- Wanting to have the body parts of another gender
- Wanting to be a different gender than the sex assigned at birth
- Wanting to be treated as a different gender
- Feeling or reacting that is typical for a different gender

Did the feeling have a negative impact? If so, how did it impact you?
- On my emotional health
- On my friends, family, or social life
- On my work or education
- On my self-care (diet, sleep, hygiene, exercise)
- No negative impact

Write out your thoughts:

Date:_____ Time:_____

Is the feeling good or bad?

How strong is the feeling? (Circle a number)

1   2   3   4   5   6   7   8   9   10

How would you categorize this feeling?
- ◯ Difference between the gender I feel I am and the sex I was assigned at birth
- ◯ Wanting to remove or change my body parts
- ◯ Wanting to have the body parts of another gender
- ◯ Wanting to be a different gender than the sex assigned at birth
- ◯ Wanting to be treated as a different gender
- ◯ Feeling or reacting that is typical for a different gender

Did the feeling have a negative impact? If so, how did it impact you?
- ◯ On my emotional health
- ◯ On my friends, family, or social life
- ◯ On my work or education
- ◯ On my self-care (diet, sleep, hygiene, exercise)
- ◯ No negative impact

Write out your thoughts:

Date:_____ Time:_____

Is the feeling good or bad?

How strong is the feeling? (Circle a number)

1   2   3   4   5   6   7   8   9   10

How would you categorize this feeling?
- ○ Difference between the gender I feel I am and the sex I was assigned at birth
- ○ Wanting to remove or change my body parts
- ○ Wanting to have the body parts of another gender
- ○ Wanting to be a different gender than the sex assigned at birth
- ○ Wanting to be treated as a different gender
- ○ Feeling or reacting that is typical for a different gender

Did the feeling have a negative impact? If so, how did it impact you?
- ○ On my emotional health
- ○ On my friends, family, or social life
- ○ On my work or education
- ○ On my self-care (diet, sleep, hygiene, exercise)
- ○ No negative impact

Write out your thoughts:

Date:_____ Time:_____

Is the feeling good or bad?

How strong is the feeling? (Circle a number)

1   2   3   4   5   6   7   8   9   10

How would you categorize this feeling?
- Difference between the gender I feel I am and the sex I was assigned at birth
- Wanting to remove or change my body parts
- Wanting to have the body parts of another gender
- Wanting to be a different gender than the sex assigned at birth
- Wanting to be treated as a different gender
- Feeling or reacting that is typical for a different gender

Did the feeling have a negative impact? If so, how did it impact you?
- On my emotional health
- On my friends, family, or social life
- On my work or education
- On my self-care (diet, sleep, hygiene, exercise)
- No negative impact

Write out your thoughts:

Date:_____ **Time:**_____

Is the feeling good or bad?

How strong is the feeling? (Circle a number)

1 2 3 4 5 6 7 8 9 10

How would you categorize this feeling?
- Difference between the gender I feel I am and the sex I was assigned at birth
- Wanting to remove or change my body parts
- Wanting to have the body parts of another gender
- Wanting to be a different gender than the sex assigned at birth
- Wanting to be treated as a different gender
- Feeling or reacting that is typical for a different gender

Did the feeling have a negative impact? If so, how did it impact you?
- On my emotional health
- On my friends, family, or social life
- On my work or education
- On my self-care (diet, sleep, hygiene, exercise)
- No negative impact

Write out your thoughts:

Date:_____ Time:_____

Is the feeling good or bad?

How strong is the feeling? (Circle a number)

1   2   3   4   5   6   7   8   9   10

How would you categorize this feeling?
- Difference between the gender I feel I am and the sex I was assigned at birth
- Wanting to remove or change my body parts
- Wanting to have the body parts of another gender
- Wanting to be a different gender than the sex assigned at birth
- Wanting to be treated as a different gender
- Feeling or reacting that is typical for a different gender

Did the feeling have a negative impact? If so, how did it impact you?
- On my emotional health
- On my friends, family, or social life
- On my work or education
- On my self-care (diet, sleep, hygiene, exercise)
- No negative impact

Write out your thoughts:

Date:_____ Time:_____

Is the feeling good or bad?

How strong is the feeling? (Circle a number)

1   2   3   4   5   6   7   8   9   10

How would you categorize this feeling?

- ○ Difference between the gender I feel I am and the sex I was assigned at birth
- ○ Wanting to remove or change my body parts
- ○ Wanting to have the body parts of another gender
- ○ Wanting to be a different gender than the sex assigned at birth
- ○ Wanting to be treated as a different gender
- ○ Feeling or reacting that is typical for a different gender

Did the feeling have a negative impact? If so, how did it impact you?

- ○ On my emotional health
- ○ On my friends, family, or social life
- ○ On my work or education
- ○ On my self-care (diet, sleep, hygiene, exercise)
- ○ No negative impact

Write out your thoughts:

Date:_____ Time:_____

Is the feeling good or bad?

How strong is the feeling? (Circle a number)

1   2   3   4   5   6   7   8   9   10

How would you categorize this feeling?
- ○ Difference between the gender I feel I am and the sex I was assigned at birth
- ○ Wanting to remove or change my body parts
- ○ Wanting to have the body parts of another gender
- ○ Wanting to be a different gender than the sex assigned at birth
- ○ Wanting to be treated as a different gender
- ○ Feeling or reacting that is typical for a different gender

Did the feeling have a negative impact? If so, how did it impact you?
- ○ On my emotional health
- ○ On my friends, family, or social life
- ○ On my work or education
- ○ On my self-care (diet, sleep, hygiene, exercise)
- ○ No negative impact

Write out your thoughts:

Date:_____   Time:_____

Is the feeling good or bad?

How strong is the feeling? (Circle a number)

1   2   3   4   5   6   7   8   9   10

How would you categorize this feeling?
- ○ Difference between the gender I feel I am and the sex I was assigned at birth
- ○ Wanting to remove or change my body parts
- ○ Wanting to have the body parts of another gender
- ○ Wanting to be a different gender than the sex assigned at birth
- ○ Wanting to be treated as a different gender
- ○ Feeling or reacting that is typical for a different gender

Did the feeling have a negative impact? If so, how did it impact you?
- ○ On my emotional health
- ○ On my friends, family, or social life
- ○ On my work or education
- ○ On my self-care (diet, sleep, hygiene, exercise)
- ○ No negative impact

Write out your thoughts:

Date:_____ Time:_____

Is the feeling good or bad?

How strong is the feeling? (Circle a number)

1 2 3 4 5 6 7 8 9 10

How would you categorize this feeling?
- Difference between the gender I feel I am and the sex I was assigned at birth
- Wanting to remove or change my body parts
- Wanting to have the body parts of another gender
- Wanting to be a different gender than the sex assigned at birth
- Wanting to be treated as a different gender
- Feeling or reacting that is typical for a different gender

Did the feeling have a negative impact? If so, how did it impact you?
- On my emotional health
- On my friends, family, or social life
- On my work or education
- On my self-care (diet, sleep, hygiene, exercise)
- No negative impact

Write out your thoughts:

Date: _____ **Time:** _____

Is the feeling good or bad?

How strong is the feeling? (Circle a number)

1 2 3 4 5 6 7 8 9 10

How would you categorize this feeling?
- Difference between the gender I feel I am and the sex I was assigned at birth
- Wanting to remove or change my body parts
- Wanting to have the body parts of another gender
- Wanting to be a different gender than the sex assigned at birth
- Wanting to be treated as a different gender
- Feeling or reacting that is typical for a different gender

Did the feeling have a negative impact? If so, how did it impact you?
- On my emotional health
- On my friends, family, or social life
- On my work or education
- On my self-care (diet, sleep, hygiene, exercise)
- No negative impact

Write out your thoughts:

Date:_____ Time:_____

Is the feeling good or bad?

How strong is the feeling? (Circle a number)

1   2   3   4   5   6   7   8   9   10

How would you categorize this feeling?
- Difference between the gender I feel I am and the sex I was assigned at birth
- Wanting to remove or change my body parts
- Wanting to have the body parts of another gender
- Wanting to be a different gender than the sex assigned at birth
- Wanting to be treated as a different gender
- Feeling or reacting that is typical for a different gender

Did the feeling have a negative impact? If so, how did it impact you?
- On my emotional health
- On my friends, family, or social life
- On my work or education
- On my self-care (diet, sleep, hygiene, exercise)
- No negative impact

Write out your thoughts:

Date:_____ **Time:**_____

Is the feeling good or bad?

How strong is the feeling? (Circle a number)

1 2 3 4 5 6 7 8 9 10

How would you categorize this feeling?
- Difference between the gender I feel I am and the sex I was assigned at birth
- Wanting to remove or change my body parts
- Wanting to have the body parts of another gender
- Wanting to be a different gender than the sex assigned at birth
- Wanting to be treated as a different gender
- Feeling or reacting that is typical for a different gender

Did the feeling have a negative impact? If so, how did it impact you?
- On my emotional health
- On my friends, family, or social life
- On my work or education
- On my self-care (diet, sleep, hygiene, exercise)
- No negative impact

Write out your thoughts:

Date:_____ Time:_____

Is the feeling good or bad?

How strong is the feeling? (Circle a number)

1   2   3   4   5   6   7   8   9   10

How would you categorize this feeling?
- ○ Difference between the gender I feel I am and the sex I was assigned at birth
- ○ Wanting to remove or change my body parts
- ○ Wanting to have the body parts of another gender
- ○ Wanting to be a different gender than the sex assigned at birth
- ○ Wanting to be treated as a different gender
- ○ Feeling or reacting that is typical for a different gender

Did the feeling have a negative impact? If so, how did it impact you?
- ○ On my emotional health
- ○ On my friends, family, or social life
- ○ On my work or education
- ○ On my self-care (diet, sleep, hygiene, exercise)
- ○ No negative impact

Write out your thoughts:

Date:_____ **Time:**_____

Is the feeling good or bad?

How strong is the feeling? (Circle a number)
1   2   3   4   5   6   7   8   9   10

How would you categorize this feeling?
- ○ Difference between the gender I feel I am and the sex I was assigned at birth
- ○ Wanting to remove or change my body parts
- ○ Wanting to have the body parts of another gender
- ○ Wanting to be a different gender than the sex assigned at birth
- ○ Wanting to be treated as a different gender
- ○ Feeling or reacting that is typical for a different gender

Did the feeling have a negative impact? If so, how did it impact you?
- ○ On my emotional health
- ○ On my friends, family, or social life
- ○ On my work or education
- ○ On my self-care (diet, sleep, hygiene, exercise)
- ○ No negative impact

Write out your thoughts:

Date:_____ Time:_____

Is the feeling good or bad?

How strong is the feeling? (Circle a number)

1   2   3   4   5   6   7   8   9   10

How would you categorize this feeling?
- Difference between the gender I feel I am and the sex I was assigned at birth
- Wanting to remove or change my body parts
- Wanting to have the body parts of another gender
- Wanting to be a different gender than the sex assigned at birth
- Wanting to be treated as a different gender
- Feeling or reacting that is typical for a different gender

Did the feeling have a negative impact? If so, how did it impact you?
- On my emotional health
- On my friends, family, or social life
- On my work or education
- On my self-care (diet, sleep, hygiene, exercise)
- No negative impact

Write out your thoughts:

Date:_____ Time:_____

Is the feeling good or bad?

How strong is the feeling? (Circle a number)

1 2 3 4 5 6 7 8 9 10

How would you categorize this feeling?
- Difference between the gender I feel I am and the sex I was assigned at birth
- Wanting to remove or change my body parts
- Wanting to have the body parts of another gender
- Wanting to be a different gender than the sex assigned at birth
- Wanting to be treated as a different gender
- Feeling or reacting that is typical for a different gender

Did the feeling have a negative impact? If so, how did it impact you?
- On my emotional health
- On my friends, family, or social life
- On my work or education
- On my self-care (diet, sleep, hygiene, exercise)
- No negative impact

Write out your thoughts:

Date:_____ Time:_____

Is the feeling good or bad?

How strong is the feeling? (Circle a number)

1   2   3   4   5   6   7   8   9   10

How would you categorize this feeling?
- Difference between the gender I feel I am and the sex I was assigned at birth
- Wanting to remove or change my body parts
- Wanting to have the body parts of another gender
- Wanting to be a different gender than the sex assigned at birth
- Wanting to be treated as a different gender
- Feeling or reacting that is typical for a different gender

Did the feeling have a negative impact? If so, how did it impact you?
- On my emotional health
- On my friends, family, or social life
- On my work or education
- On my self-care (diet, sleep, hygiene, exercise)
- No negative impact

Write out your thoughts:

Date:_____ Time:_____

Is the feeling good or bad?

How strong is the feeling? (Circle a number)

1   2   3   4   5   6   7   8   9   10

How would you categorize this feeling?
- ○ Difference between the gender I feel I am and the sex I was assigned at birth
- ○ Wanting to remove or change my body parts
- ○ Wanting to have the body parts of another gender
- ○ Wanting to be a different gender than the sex assigned at birth
- ○ Wanting to be treated as a different gender
- ○ Feeling or reacting that is typical for a different gender

Did the feeling have a negative impact? If so, how did it impact you?
- ○ On my emotional health
- ○ On my friends, family, or social life
- ○ On my work or education
- ○ On my self-care (diet, sleep, hygiene, exercise)
- ○ No negative impact

Write out your thoughts:

Date:_____ Time:_____

Is the feeling good or bad?

How strong is the feeling? (Circle a number)

1   2   3   4   5   6   7   8   9   10

How would you categorize this feeling?

- Difference between the gender I feel I am and the sex I was assigned at birth
- Wanting to remove or change my body parts
- Wanting to have the body parts of another gender
- Wanting to be a different gender than the sex assigned at birth
- Wanting to be treated as a different gender
- Feeling or reacting that is typical for a different gender

Did the feeling have a negative impact? If so, how did it impact you?

- On my emotional health
- On my friends, family, or social life
- On my work or education
- On my self-care (diet, sleep, hygiene, exercise)
- No negative impact

Write out your thoughts:

Date:_____ Time:_____

Is the feeling good or bad?

How strong is the feeling? (Circle a number)

1   2   3   4   5   6   7   8   9   10

How would you categorize this feeling?

- Difference between the gender I feel I am and the sex I was assigned at birth
- Wanting to remove or change my body parts
- Wanting to have the body parts of another gender
- Wanting to be a different gender than the sex assigned at birth
- Wanting to be treated as a different gender
- Feeling or reacting that is typical for a different gender

Did the feeling have a negative impact? If so, how did it impact you?

- On my emotional health
- On my friends, family, or social life
- On my work or education
- On my self-care (diet, sleep, hygiene, exercise)
- No negative impact

Write out your thoughts:

Date:_____ **Time:**_____

Is the feeling good or bad?

How strong is the feeling? (Circle a number)

1 2 3 4 5 6 7 8 9 10

How would you categorize this feeling?
- Difference between the gender I feel I am and the sex I was assigned at birth
- Wanting to remove or change my body parts
- Wanting to have the body parts of another gender
- Wanting to be a different gender than the sex assigned at birth
- Wanting to be treated as a different gender
- Feeling or reacting that is typical for a different gender

Did the feeling have a negative impact? If so, how did it impact you?
- On my emotional health
- On my friends, family, or social life
- On my work or education
- On my self-care (diet, sleep, hygiene, exercise)
- No negative impact

Write out your thoughts:

Date:_____ Time:_____

Is the feeling good or bad?

How strong is the feeling? (Circle a number)

1   2   3   4   5   6   7   8   9   10

How would you categorize this feeling?
- Difference between the gender I feel I am and the sex I was assigned at birth
- Wanting to remove or change my body parts
- Wanting to have the body parts of another gender
- Wanting to be a different gender than the sex assigned at birth
- Wanting to be treated as a different gender
- Feeling or reacting that is typical for a different gender

Did the feeling have a negative impact? If so, how did it impact you?
- On my emotional health
- On my friends, family, or social life
- On my work or education
- On my self-care (diet, sleep, hygiene, exercise)
- No negative impact

Write out your thoughts:

Date:_____ Time:_____

Is the feeling good or bad?

How strong is the feeling? (Circle a number)

1 2 3 4 5 6 7 8 9 10

How would you categorize this feeling?

- ○ Difference between the gender I feel I am and the sex I was assigned at birth
- ○ Wanting to remove or change my body parts
- ○ Wanting to have the body parts of another gender
- ○ Wanting to be a different gender than the sex assigned at birth
- ○ Wanting to be treated as a different gender
- ○ Feeling or reacting that is typical for a different gender

Did the feeling have a negative impact? If so, how did it impact you?

- ○ On my emotional health
- ○ On my friends, family, or social life
- ○ On my work or education
- ○ On my self-care (diet, sleep, hygiene, exercise)
- ○ No negative impact

Write out your thoughts:

Date:_____ **Time:**_____

Is the feeling good or bad?

How strong is the feeling? (Circle a number)

1   2   3   4   5   6   7   8   9   10

How would you categorize this feeling?
- Difference between the gender I feel I am and the sex I was assigned at birth
- Wanting to remove or change my body parts
- Wanting to have the body parts of another gender
- Wanting to be a different gender than the sex assigned at birth
- Wanting to be treated as a different gender
- Feeling or reacting that is typical for a different gender

Did the feeling have a negative impact? If so, how did it impact you?
- On my emotional health
- On my friends, family, or social life
- On my work or education
- On my self-care (diet, sleep, hygiene, exercise)
- No negative impact

Write out your thoughts:

Date:_____ Time:_____

Is the feeling good or bad?

How strong is the feeling? (Circle a number)

1   2   3   4   5   6   7   8   9   10

How would you categorize this feeling?
- ○ Difference between the gender I feel I am and the sex I was assigned at birth
- ○ Wanting to remove or change my body parts
- ○ Wanting to have the body parts of another gender
- ○ Wanting to be a different gender than the sex assigned at birth
- ○ Wanting to be treated as a different gender
- ○ Feeling or reacting that is typical for a different gender

Did the feeling have a negative impact? If so, how did it impact you?
- ○ On my emotional health
- ○ On my friends, family, or social life
- ○ On my work or education
- ○ On my self-care (diet, sleep, hygiene, exercise)
- ○ No negative impact

Write out your thoughts:

Date:_____ **Time:**_____

Is the feeling good or bad?

How strong is the feeling? (Circle a number)

1 2 3 4 5 6 7 8 9 10

How would you categorize this feeling?
- Difference between the gender I feel I am and the sex I was assigned at birth
- Wanting to remove or change my body parts
- Wanting to have the body parts of another gender
- Wanting to be a different gender than the sex assigned at birth
- Wanting to be treated as a different gender
- Feeling or reacting that is typical for a different gender

Did the feeling have a negative impact? If so, how did it impact you?
- On my emotional health
- On my friends, family, or social life
- On my work or education
- On my self-care (diet, sleep, hygiene, exercise)
- No negative impact

Write out your thoughts:

Date:_____ Time:_____

Is the feeling good or bad?

How strong is the feeling? (Circle a number)

1 2 3 4 5 6 7 8 9 10

How would you categorize this feeling?
- Difference between the gender I feel I am and the sex I was assigned at birth
- Wanting to remove or change my body parts
- Wanting to have the body parts of another gender
- Wanting to be a different gender than the sex assigned at birth
- Wanting to be treated as a different gender
- Feeling or reacting that is typical for a different gender

Did the feeling have a negative impact? If so, how did it impact you?
- On my emotional health
- On my friends, family, or social life
- On my work or education
- On my self-care (diet, sleep, hygiene, exercise)
- No negative impact

Write out your thoughts:

Date:_____ Time:_____

Is the feeling good or bad?

How strong is the feeling? (Circle a number)

1   2   3   4   5   6   7   8   9   10

How would you categorize this feeling?

- Difference between the gender I feel I am and the sex I was assigned at birth
- Wanting to remove or change my body parts
- Wanting to have the body parts of another gender
- Wanting to be a different gender than the sex assigned at birth
- Wanting to be treated as a different gender
- Feeling or reacting that is typical for a different gender

Did the feeling have a negative impact? If so, how did it impact you?

- On my emotional health
- On my friends, family, or social life
- On my work or education
- On my self-care (diet, sleep, hygiene, exercise)
- No negative impact

Write out your thoughts:

Date:_____ Time:_____

Is the feeling good or bad?

How strong is the feeling? (Circle a number)

1   2   3   4   5   6   7   8   9   10

How would you categorize this feeling?
- Difference between the gender I feel I am and the sex I was assigned at birth
- Wanting to remove or change my body parts
- Wanting to have the body parts of another gender
- Wanting to be a different gender than the sex assigned at birth
- Wanting to be treated as a different gender
- Feeling or reacting that is typical for a different gender

Did the feeling have a negative impact? If so, how did it impact you?
- On my emotional health
- On my friends, family, or social life
- On my work or education
- On my self-care (diet, sleep, hygiene, exercise)
- No negative impact

Write out your thoughts:

Date:_____ Time:_____

Is the feeling good or bad?

How strong is the feeling? (Circle a number)

1 2 3 4 5 6 7 8 9 10

How would you categorize this feeling?
- ○ Difference between the gender I feel I am and the sex I was assigned at birth
- ○ Wanting to remove or change my body parts
- ○ Wanting to have the body parts of another gender
- ○ Wanting to be a different gender than the sex assigned at birth
- ○ Wanting to be treated as a different gender
- ○ Feeling or reacting that is typical for a different gender

Did the feeling have a negative impact? If so, how did it impact you?
- ○ On my emotional health
- ○ On my friends, family, or social life
- ○ On my work or education
- ○ On my self-care (diet, sleep, hygiene, exercise)
- ○ No negative impact

Write out your thoughts:

Date:_____ Time:_____

Is the feeling good or bad?

How strong is the feeling? (Circle a number)

1   2   3   4   5   6   7   8   9   10

How would you categorize this feeling?
- Difference between the gender I feel I am and the sex I was assigned at birth
- Wanting to remove or change my body parts
- Wanting to have the body parts of another gender
- Wanting to be a different gender than the sex assigned at birth
- Wanting to be treated as a different gender
- Feeling or reacting that is typical for a different gender

Did the feeling have a negative impact? If so, how did it impact you?
- On my emotional health
- On my friends, family, or social life
- On my work or education
- On my self-care (diet, sleep, hygiene, exercise)
- No negative impact

Write out your thoughts:

Date:_____ **Time:**_____

Is the feeling good or bad?

How strong is the feeling? (Circle a number)

1   2   3   4   5   6   7   8   9   10

How would you categorize this feeling?
- Difference between the gender I feel I am and the sex I was assigned at birth
- Wanting to remove or change my body parts
- Wanting to have the body parts of another gender
- Wanting to be a different gender than the sex assigned at birth
- Wanting to be treated as a different gender
- Feeling or reacting that is typical for a different gender

Did the feeling have a negative impact? If so, how did it impact you?
- On my emotional health
- On my friends, family, or social life
- On my work or education
- On my self-care (diet, sleep, hygiene, exercise)
- No negative impact

Write out your thoughts:

Date:_____ **Time:**_____

Is the feeling good or bad?

How strong is the feeling? (Circle a number)

1   2   3   4   5   6   7   8   9   10

How would you categorize this feeling?
- Difference between the gender I feel I am and the sex I was assigned at birth
- Wanting to remove or change my body parts
- Wanting to have the body parts of another gender
- Wanting to be a different gender than the sex assigned at birth
- Wanting to be treated as a different gender
- Feeling or reacting that is typical for a different gender

Did the feeling have a negative impact? If so, how did it impact you?
- On my emotional health
- On my friends, family, or social life
- On my work or education
- On my self-care (diet, sleep, hygiene, exercise)
- No negative impact

Write out your thoughts:

Date:_____ Time:_____

Is the feeling good or bad?

How strong is the feeling? (Circle a number)

1 2 3 4 5 6 7 8 9 10

How would you categorize this feeling?

- ○ Difference between the gender I feel I am and the sex I was assigned at birth
- ○ Wanting to remove or change my body parts
- ○ Wanting to have the body parts of another gender
- ○ Wanting to be a different gender than the sex assigned at birth
- ○ Wanting to be treated as a different gender
- ○ Feeling or reacting that is typical for a different gender

Did the feeling have a negative impact? If so, how did it impact you?

- ○ On my emotional health
- ○ On my friends, family, or social life
- ○ On my work or education
- ○ On my self-care (diet, sleep, hygiene, exercise)
- ○ No negative impact

Write out your thoughts:

Date:_____ Time:_____

Is the feeling good or bad?

How strong is the feeling? (Circle a number)

1   2   3   4   5   6   7   8   9   10

How would you categorize this feeling?

- Difference between the gender I feel I am and the sex I was assigned at birth
- Wanting to remove or change my body parts
- Wanting to have the body parts of another gender
- Wanting to be a different gender than the sex assigned at birth
- Wanting to be treated as a different gender
- Feeling or reacting that is typical for a different gender

Did the feeling have a negative impact? If so, how did it impact you?

- On my emotional health
- On my friends, family, or social life
- On my work or education
- On my self-care (diet, sleep, hygiene, exercise)
- No negative impact

Write out your thoughts:

Date:_____   Time:_____

Is the feeling good or bad?

How strong is the feeling? (Circle a number)

1   2   3   4   5   6   7   8   9   10

How would you categorize this feeling?
- ○ Difference between the gender I feel I am and the sex I was assigned at birth
- ○ Wanting to remove or change my body parts
- ○ Wanting to have the body parts of another gender
- ○ Wanting to be a different gender than the sex assigned at birth
- ○ Wanting to be treated as a different gender
- ○ Feeling or reacting that is typical for a different gender

Did the feeling have a negative impact? If so, how did it impact you?
- ○ On my emotional health
- ○ On my friends, family, or social life
- ○ On my work or education
- ○ On my self-care (diet, sleep, hygiene, exercise)
- ○ No negative impact

Write out your thoughts:

Date:_____ Time:_____

Is the feeling good or bad?

How strong is the feeling? (Circle a number)

1   2   3   4   5   6   7   8   9   10

How would you categorize this feeling?
- Difference between the gender I feel I am and the sex I was assigned at birth
- Wanting to remove or change my body parts
- Wanting to have the body parts of another gender
- Wanting to be a different gender than the sex assigned at birth
- Wanting to be treated as a different gender
- Feeling or reacting that is typical for a different gender

Did the feeling have a negative impact? If so, how did it impact you?
- On my emotional health
- On my friends, family, or social life
- On my work or education
- On my self-care (diet, sleep, hygiene, exercise)
- No negative impact

Write out your thoughts:

Date:_____ **Time:**_____

Is the feeling good or bad?

How strong is the feeling? (Circle a number)

1   2   3   4   5   6   7   8   9   10

How would you categorize this feeling?
- Difference between the gender I feel I am and the sex I was assigned at birth
- Wanting to remove or change my body parts
- Wanting to have the body parts of another gender
- Wanting to be a different gender than the sex assigned at birth
- Wanting to be treated as a different gender
- Feeling or reacting that is typical for a different gender

Did the feeling have a negative impact? If so, how did it impact you?
- On my emotional health
- On my friends, family, or social life
- On my work or education
- On my self-care (diet, sleep, hygiene, exercise)
- No negative impact

Write out your thoughts:

Date:_____ Time:_____

Is the feeling good or bad?

How strong is the feeling? (Circle a number)

1 2 3 4 5 6 7 8 9 10

How would you categorize this feeling?
- Difference between the gender I feel I am and the sex I was assigned at birth
- Wanting to remove or change my body parts
- Wanting to have the body parts of another gender
- Wanting to be a different gender than the sex assigned at birth
- Wanting to be treated as a different gender
- Feeling or reacting that is typical for a different gender

Did the feeling have a negative impact? If so, how did it impact you?
- On my emotional health
- On my friends, family, or social life
- On my work or education
- On my self-care (diet, sleep, hygiene, exercise)
- No negative impact

Write out your thoughts:

Date:_____ Time:_____

Is the feeling good or bad?

How strong is the feeling? (Circle a number)

1   2   3   4   5   6   7   8   9   10

How would you categorize this feeling?
- Difference between the gender I feel I am and the sex I was assigned at birth
- Wanting to remove or change my body parts
- Wanting to have the body parts of another gender
- Wanting to be a different gender than the sex assigned at birth
- Wanting to be treated as a different gender
- Feeling or reacting that is typical for a different gender

Did the feeling have a negative impact? If so, how did it impact you?
- On my emotional health
- On my friends, family, or social life
- On my work or education
- On my self-care (diet, sleep, hygiene, exercise)
- No negative impact

Write out your thoughts:

Date:_____ Time:_____

Is the feeling good or bad?

How strong is the feeling? (Circle a number)

1 2 3 4 5 6 7 8 9 10

How would you categorize this feeling?

- ○ Difference between the gender I feel I am and the sex I was assigned at birth
- ○ Wanting to remove or change my body parts
- ○ Wanting to have the body parts of another gender
- ○ Wanting to be a different gender than the sex assigned at birth
- ○ Wanting to be treated as a different gender
- ○ Feeling or reacting that is typical for a different gender

Did the feeling have a negative impact? If so, how did it impact you?

- ○ On my emotional health
- ○ On my friends, family, or social life
- ○ On my work or education
- ○ On my self-care (diet, sleep, hygiene, exercise)
- ○ No negative impact

Write out your thoughts:

Date:_____ Time:_____

Is the feeling good or bad?

How strong is the feeling? (Circle a number)

1   2   3   4   5   6   7   8   9   10

How would you categorize this feeling?
- Difference between the gender I feel I am and the sex I was assigned at birth
- Wanting to remove or change my body parts
- Wanting to have the body parts of another gender
- Wanting to be a different gender than the sex assigned at birth
- Wanting to be treated as a different gender
- Feeling or reacting that is typical for a different gender

Did the feeling have a negative impact? If so, how did it impact you?
- On my emotional health
- On my friends, family, or social life
- On my work or education
- On my self-care (diet, sleep, hygiene, exercise)
- No negative impact

Write out your thoughts:

Date:_____ Time:_____

Is the feeling good or bad?

How strong is the feeling? (Circle a number)

1   2   3   4   5   6   7   8   9   10

How would you categorize this feeling?
- Difference between the gender I feel I am and the sex I was assigned at birth
- Wanting to remove or change my body parts
- Wanting to have the body parts of another gender
- Wanting to be a different gender than the sex assigned at birth
- Wanting to be treated as a different gender
- Feeling or reacting that is typical for a different gender

Did the feeling have a negative impact? If so, how did it impact you?
- On my emotional health
- On my friends, family, or social life
- On my work or education
- On my self-care (diet, sleep, hygiene, exercise)
- No negative impact

Write out your thoughts:

Date:_____ Time:_____

Is the feeling good or bad?

How strong is the feeling? (Circle a number)

1 2 3 4 5 6 7 8 9 10

How would you categorize this feeling?

- ○ Difference between the gender I feel I am and the sex I was assigned at birth
- ○ Wanting to remove or change my body parts
- ○ Wanting to have the body parts of another gender
- ○ Wanting to be a different gender than the sex assigned at birth
- ○ Wanting to be treated as a different gender
- ○ Feeling or reacting that is typical for a different gender

Did the feeling have a negative impact? If so, how did it impact you?

- ○ On my emotional health
- ○ On my friends, family, or social life
- ○ On my work or education
- ○ On my self-care (diet, sleep, hygiene, exercise)
- ○ No negative impact

Write out your thoughts:

Date:_____   Time:_____

Is the feeling good or bad?

How strong is the feeling? (Circle a number)

1 2 3 4 5 6 7 8 9 10

How would you categorize this feeling?
- Difference between the gender I feel I am and the sex I was assigned at birth
- Wanting to remove or change my body parts
- Wanting to have the body parts of another gender
- Wanting to be a different gender than the sex assigned at birth
- Wanting to be treated as a different gender
- Feeling or reacting that is typical for a different gender

Did the feeling have a negative impact? If so, how did it impact you?
- On my emotional health
- On my friends, family, or social life
- On my work or education
- On my self-care (diet, sleep, hygiene, exercise)
- No negative impact

Write out your thoughts:

Date:_____ Time:_____

Is the feeling good or bad?

How strong is the feeling? (Circle a number)

1 2 3 4 5 6 7 8 9 10

How would you categorize this feeling?
- ○ Difference between the gender I feel I am and the sex I was assigned at birth
- ○ Wanting to remove or change my body parts
- ○ Wanting to have the body parts of another gender
- ○ Wanting to be a different gender than the sex assigned at birth
- ○ Wanting to be treated as a different gender
- ○ Feeling or reacting that is typical for a different gender

Did the feeling have a negative impact? If so, how did it impact you?
- ○ On my emotional health
- ○ On my friends, family, or social life
- ○ On my work or education
- ○ On my self-care (diet, sleep, hygiene, exercise)
- ○ No negative impact

Write out your thoughts:

Date:_____ Time:_____

Is the feeling good or bad?

How strong is the feeling? (Circle a number)

1 2 3 4 5 6 7 8 9 10

How would you categorize this feeling?
- Difference between the gender I feel I am and the sex I was assigned at birth
- Wanting to remove or change my body parts
- Wanting to have the body parts of another gender
- Wanting to be a different gender than the sex assigned at birth
- Wanting to be treated as a different gender
- Feeling or reacting that is typical for a different gender

Did the feeling have a negative impact? If so, how did it impact you?
- On my emotional health
- On my friends, family, or social life
- On my work or education
- On my self-care (diet, sleep, hygiene, exercise)
- No negative impact

Write out your thoughts:

Date:_____ Time:_____

Is the feeling good or bad?

How strong is the feeling? (Circle a number)

1 2 3 4 5 6 7 8 9 10

How would you categorize this feeling?
- Difference between the gender I feel I am and the sex I was assigned at birth
- Wanting to remove or change my body parts
- Wanting to have the body parts of another gender
- Wanting to be a different gender than the sex assigned at birth
- Wanting to be treated as a different gender
- Feeling or reacting that is typical for a different gender

Did the feeling have a negative impact? If so, how did it impact you?
- On my emotional health
- On my friends, family, or social life
- On my work or education
- On my self-care (diet, sleep, hygiene, exercise)
- No negative impact

Write out your thoughts:

Date:_____   Time:_____

Is the feeling good or bad?

How strong is the feeling? (Circle a number)

1   2   3   4   5   6   7   8   9   10

How would you categorize this feeling?

- Difference between the gender I feel I am and the sex I was assigned at birth
- Wanting to remove or change my body parts
- Wanting to have the body parts of another gender
- Wanting to be a different gender than the sex assigned at birth
- Wanting to be treated as a different gender
- Feeling or reacting that is typical for a different gender

Did the feeling have a negative impact? If so, how did it impact you?

- On my emotional health
- On my friends, family, or social life
- On my work or education
- On my self-care (diet, sleep, hygiene, exercise)
- No negative impact

Write out your thoughts:

Date:_____ Time:_____

Is the feeling good or bad?

How strong is the feeling? (Circle a number)

1   2   3   4   5   6   7   8   9   10

How would you categorize this feeling?
- Difference between the gender I feel I am and the sex I was assigned at birth
- Wanting to remove or change my body parts
- Wanting to have the body parts of another gender
- Wanting to be a different gender than the sex assigned at birth
- Wanting to be treated as a different gender
- Feeling or reacting that is typical for a different gender

Did the feeling have a negative impact? If so, how did it impact you?
- On my emotional health
- On my friends, family, or social life
- On my work or education
- On my self-care (diet, sleep, hygiene, exercise)
- No negative impact

Write out your thoughts:

Date:_____ Time:_____

Is the feeling good or bad?

How strong is the feeling? (Circle a number)

1   2   3   4   5   6   7   8   9   10

How would you categorize this feeling?
- Difference between the gender I feel I am and the sex I was assigned at birth
- Wanting to remove or change my body parts
- Wanting to have the body parts of another gender
- Wanting to be a different gender than the sex assigned at birth
- Wanting to be treated as a different gender
- Feeling or reacting that is typical for a different gender

Did the feeling have a negative impact? If so, how did it impact you?
- On my emotional health
- On my friends, family, or social life
- On my work or education
- On my self-care (diet, sleep, hygiene, exercise)
- No negative impact

Write out your thoughts:

Date:_____ **Time:**_____

Is the feeling good or bad?

How strong is the feeling? (Circle a number)

1   2   3   4   5   6   7   8   9   10

How would you categorize this feeling?
- Difference between the gender I feel I am and the sex I was assigned at birth
- Wanting to remove or change my body parts
- Wanting to have the body parts of another gender
- Wanting to be a different gender than the sex assigned at birth
- Wanting to be treated as a different gender
- Feeling or reacting that is typical for a different gender

Did the feeling have a negative impact? If so, how did it impact you?
- On my emotional health
- On my friends, family, or social life
- On my work or education
- On my self-care (diet, sleep, hygiene, exercise)
- No negative impact

Write out your thoughts:

Date:_____ Time:_____

Is the feeling good or bad?

How strong is the feeling? (Circle a number)

1   2   3   4   5   6   7   8   9   10

How would you categorize this feeling?
- Difference between the gender I feel I am and the sex I was assigned at birth
- Wanting to remove or change my body parts
- Wanting to have the body parts of another gender
- Wanting to be a different gender than the sex assigned at birth
- Wanting to be treated as a different gender
- Feeling or reacting that is typical for a different gender

Did the feeling have a negative impact? If so, how did it impact you?
- On my emotional health
- On my friends, family, or social life
- On my work or education
- On my self-care (diet, sleep, hygiene, exercise)
- No negative impact

Write out your thoughts:

Date:_____ Time:_____

Is the feeling good or bad?

How strong is the feeling? (Circle a number)

1   2   3   4   5   6   7   8   9   10

How would you categorize this feeling?
- Difference between the gender I feel I am and the sex I was assigned at birth
- Wanting to remove or change my body parts
- Wanting to have the body parts of another gender
- Wanting to be a different gender than the sex assigned at birth
- Wanting to be treated as a different gender
- Feeling or reacting that is typical for a different gender

Did the feeling have a negative impact? If so, how did it impact you?
- On my emotional health
- On my friends, family, or social life
- On my work or education
- On my self-care (diet, sleep, hygiene, exercise)
- No negative impact

Write out your thoughts:

Date:_____ Time:_____

Is the feeling good or bad?

How strong is the feeling? (Circle a number)

1   2   3   4   5   6   7   8   9   10

How would you categorize this feeling?

- Difference between the gender I feel I am and the sex I was assigned at birth
- Wanting to remove or change my body parts
- Wanting to have the body parts of another gender
- Wanting to be a different gender than the sex assigned at birth
- Wanting to be treated as a different gender
- Feeling or reacting that is typical for a different gender

Did the feeling have a negative impact? If so, how did it impact you?

- On my emotional health
- On my friends, family, or social life
- On my work or education
- On my self-care (diet, sleep, hygiene, exercise)
- No negative impact

Write out your thoughts:

Date:_____ Time:_____

Is the feeling good or bad?

How strong is the feeling? (Circle a number)

1 2 3 4 5 6 7 8 9 10

How would you categorize this feeling?
- ○ Difference between the gender I feel I am and the sex I was assigned at birth
- ○ Wanting to remove or change my body parts
- ○ Wanting to have the body parts of another gender
- ○ Wanting to be a different gender than the sex assigned at birth
- ○ Wanting to be treated as a different gender
- ○ Feeling or reacting that is typical for a different gender

Did the feeling have a negative impact? If so, how did it impact you?
- ○ On my emotional health
- ○ On my friends, family, or social life
- ○ On my work or education
- ○ On my self-care (diet, sleep, hygiene, exercise)
- ○ No negative impact

Write out your thoughts:

Date:_____ Time:_____

Is the feeling good or bad?

How strong is the feeling? (Circle a number)

1   2   3   4   5   6   7   8   9   10

How would you categorize this feeling?

- ○ Difference between the gender I feel I am and the sex I was assigned at birth
- ○ Wanting to remove or change my body parts
- ○ Wanting to have the body parts of another gender
- ○ Wanting to be a different gender than the sex assigned at birth
- ○ Wanting to be treated as a different gender
- ○ Feeling or reacting that is typical for a different gender

Did the feeling have a negative impact? If so, how did it impact you?

- ○ On my emotional health
- ○ On my friends, family, or social life
- ○ On my work or education
- ○ On my self-care (diet, sleep, hygiene, exercise)
- ○ No negative impact

Write out your thoughts:

Date:_____ Time:_____

Is the feeling good or bad?

How strong is the feeling? (Circle a number)

1   2   3   4   5   6   7   8   9   10

How would you categorize this feeling?

- Difference between the gender I feel I am and the sex I was assigned at birth
- Wanting to remove or change my body parts
- Wanting to have the body parts of another gender
- Wanting to be a different gender than the sex assigned at birth
- Wanting to be treated as a different gender
- Feeling or reacting that is typical for a different gender

Did the feeling have a negative impact? If so, how did it impact you?

- On my emotional health
- On my friends, family, or social life
- On my work or education
- On my self-care (diet, sleep, hygiene, exercise)
- No negative impact

Write out your thoughts:

Date:_____ Time:_____

Is the feeling good or bad?

How strong is the feeling? (Circle a number)

1　2　3　4　5　6　7　8　9　10

How would you categorize this feeling?

- ○ Difference between the gender I feel I am and the sex I was assigned at birth
- ○ Wanting to remove or change my body parts
- ○ Wanting to have the body parts of another gender
- ○ Wanting to be a different gender than the sex assigned at birth
- ○ Wanting to be treated as a different gender
- ○ Feeling or reacting that is typical for a different gender

Did the feeling have a negative impact? If so, how did it impact you?

- ○ On my emotional health
- ○ On my friends, family, or social life
- ○ On my work or education
- ○ On my self-care (diet, sleep, hygiene, exercise)
- ○ No negative impact

Write out your thoughts:

Date:_____ Time:_____

Is the feeling good or bad?

How strong is the feeling? (Circle a number)

1   2   3   4   5   6   7   8   9   10

How would you categorize this feeling?

- ○ Difference between the gender I feel I am and the sex I was assigned at birth
- ○ Wanting to remove or change my body parts
- ○ Wanting to have the body parts of another gender
- ○ Wanting to be a different gender than the sex assigned at birth
- ○ Wanting to be treated as a different gender
- ○ Feeling or reacting that is typical for a different gender

Did the feeling have a negative impact? If so, how did it impact you?

- ○ On my emotional health
- ○ On my friends, family, or social life
- ○ On my work or education
- ○ On my self-care (diet, sleep, hygiene, exercise)
- ○ No negative impact

Write out your thoughts:

Date:_____ Time:_____

Is the feeling good or bad?

How strong is the feeling? (Circle a number)

1 2 3 4 5 6 7 8 9 10

How would you categorize this feeling?

- ○ Difference between the gender I feel I am and the sex I was assigned at birth
- ○ Wanting to remove or change my body parts
- ○ Wanting to have the body parts of another gender
- ○ Wanting to be a different gender than the sex assigned at birth
- ○ Wanting to be treated as a different gender
- ○ Feeling or reacting that is typical for a different gender

Did the feeling have a negative impact? If so, how did it impact you?

- ○ On my emotional health
- ○ On my friends, family, or social life
- ○ On my work or education
- ○ On my self-care (diet, sleep, hygiene, exercise)
- ○ No negative impact

Write out your thoughts:

Date:_____ Time:_____

Is the feeling good or bad?

How strong is the feeling? (Circle a number)

1　2　3　4　5　6　7　8　9　10

How would you categorize this feeling?

- ○ Difference between the gender I feel I am and the sex I was assigned at birth
- ○ Wanting to remove or change my body parts
- ○ Wanting to have the body parts of another gender
- ○ Wanting to be a different gender than the sex assigned at birth
- ○ Wanting to be treated as a different gender
- ○ Feeling or reacting that is typical for a different gender

Did the feeling have a negative impact? If so, how did it impact you?

- ○ On my emotional health
- ○ On my friends, family, or social life
- ○ On my work or education
- ○ On my self-care (diet, sleep, hygiene, exercise)
- ○ No negative impact

Write out your thoughts:

Date:_____ Time:_____

Is the feeling good or bad?

How strong is the feeling? (Circle a number)

1   2   3   4   5   6   7   8   9   10

How would you categorize this feeling?
- Difference between the gender I feel I am and the sex I was assigned at birth
- Wanting to remove or change my body parts
- Wanting to have the body parts of another gender
- Wanting to be a different gender than the sex assigned at birth
- Wanting to be treated as a different gender
- Feeling or reacting that is typical for a different gender

Did the feeling have a negative impact? If so, how did it impact you?
- On my emotional health
- On my friends, family, or social life
- On my work or education
- On my self-care (diet, sleep, hygiene, exercise)
- No negative impact

Write out your thoughts:

Date:_____ Time:_____

Is the feeling good or bad?

How strong is the feeling? (Circle a number)

1   2   3   4   5   6   7   8   9   10

How would you categorize this feeling?

- ◯ Difference between the gender I feel I am and the sex I was assigned at birth
- ◯ Wanting to remove or change my body parts
- ◯ Wanting to have the body parts of another gender
- ◯ Wanting to be a different gender than the sex assigned at birth
- ◯ Wanting to be treated as a different gender
- ◯ Feeling or reacting that is typical for a different gender

Did the feeling have a negative impact? If so, how did it impact you?

- ◯ On my emotional health
- ◯ On my friends, family, or social life
- ◯ On my work or education
- ◯ On my self-care (diet, sleep, hygiene, exercise)
- ◯ No negative impact

Write out your thoughts:

Date:_____ Time:_____

Is the feeling good or bad?

How strong is the feeling? (Circle a number)

1   2   3   4   5   6   7   8   9   10

How would you categorize this feeling?
- Difference between the gender I feel I am and the sex I was assigned at birth
- Wanting to remove or change my body parts
- Wanting to have the body parts of another gender
- Wanting to be a different gender than the sex assigned at birth
- Wanting to be treated as a different gender
- Feeling or reacting that is typical for a different gender

Did the feeling have a negative impact? If so, how did it impact you?
- On my emotional health
- On my friends, family, or social life
- On my work or education
- On my self-care (diet, sleep, hygiene, exercise)
- No negative impact

Write out your thoughts:

Date:_____ Time:_____

Is the feeling good or bad?

How strong is the feeling? (Circle a number)

1   2   3   4   5   6   7   8   9   10

How would you categorize this feeling?

- ○ Difference between the gender I feel I am and the sex I was assigned at birth
- ○ Wanting to remove or change my body parts
- ○ Wanting to have the body parts of another gender
- ○ Wanting to be a different gender than the sex assigned at birth
- ○ Wanting to be treated as a different gender
- ○ Feeling or reacting that is typical for a different gender

Did the feeling have a negative impact? If so, how did it impact you?

- ○ On my emotional health
- ○ On my friends, family, or social life
- ○ On my work or education
- ○ On my self-care (diet, sleep, hygiene, exercise)
- ○ No negative impact

Write out your thoughts:

Date:_____ Time:_____

Is the feeling good or bad?

How strong is the feeling? (Circle a number)

1   2   3   4   5   6   7   8   9   10

How would you categorize this feeling?
- Difference between the gender I feel I am and the sex I was assigned at birth
- Wanting to remove or change my body parts
- Wanting to have the body parts of another gender
- Wanting to be a different gender than the sex assigned at birth
- Wanting to be treated as a different gender
- Feeling or reacting that is typical for a different gender

Did the feeling have a negative impact? If so, how did it impact you?
- On my emotional health
- On my friends, family, or social life
- On my work or education
- On my self-care (diet, sleep, hygiene, exercise)
- No negative impact

Write out your thoughts:

Date:_____ Time:_____

Is the feeling good or bad?

How strong is the feeling? (Circle a number)

1 2 3 4 5 6 7 8 9 10

How would you categorize this feeling?

- Difference between the gender I feel I am and the sex I was assigned at birth
- Wanting to remove or change my body parts
- Wanting to have the body parts of another gender
- Wanting to be a different gender than the sex assigned at birth
- Wanting to be treated as a different gender
- Feeling or reacting that is typical for a different gender

Did the feeling have a negative impact? If so, how did it impact you?

- On my emotional health
- On my friends, family, or social life
- On my work or education
- On my self-care (diet, sleep, hygiene, exercise)
- No negative impact

Write out your thoughts:

Date:_____ Time:_____

Is the feeling good or bad?

How strong is the feeling? (Circle a number)

1 2 3 4 5 6 7 8 9 10

How would you categorize this feeling?
- Difference between the gender I feel I am and the sex I was assigned at birth
- Wanting to remove or change my body parts
- Wanting to have the body parts of another gender
- Wanting to be a different gender than the sex assigned at birth
- Wanting to be treated as a different gender
- Feeling or reacting that is typical for a different gender

Did the feeling have a negative impact? If so, how did it impact you?
- On my emotional health
- On my friends, family, or social life
- On my work or education
- On my self-care (diet, sleep, hygiene, exercise)
- No negative impact

Write out your thoughts:

Date:_____ **Time:**_____

Is the feeling good or bad?

How strong is the feeling? (Circle a number)

1   2   3   4   5   6   7   8   9   10

How would you categorize this feeling?
- Difference between the gender I feel I am and the sex I was assigned at birth
- Wanting to remove or change my body parts
- Wanting to have the body parts of another gender
- Wanting to be a different gender than the sex assigned at birth
- Wanting to be treated as a different gender
- Feeling or reacting that is typical for a different gender

Did the feeling have a negative impact? If so, how did it impact you?
- On my emotional health
- On my friends, family, or social life
- On my work or education
- On my self-care (diet, sleep, hygiene, exercise)
- No negative impact

Write out your thoughts:

Date:_____ Time:_____

Is the feeling good or bad?

How strong is the feeling? (Circle a number)

1   2   3   4   5   6   7   8   9   10

How would you categorize this feeling?

- ○ Difference between the gender I feel I am and the sex I was assigned at birth
- ○ Wanting to remove or change my body parts
- ○ Wanting to have the body parts of another gender
- ○ Wanting to be a different gender than the sex assigned at birth
- ○ Wanting to be treated as a different gender
- ○ Feeling or reacting that is typical for a different gender

Did the feeling have a negative impact? If so, how did it impact you?

- ○ On my emotional health
- ○ On my friends, family, or social life
- ○ On my work or education
- ○ On my self-care (diet, sleep, hygiene, exercise)
- ○ No negative impact

Write out your thoughts:

Date:_____   Time:_____

Is the feeling good or bad?

How strong is the feeling? (Circle a number)

1 2 3 4 5 6 7 8 9 10

How would you categorize this feeling?

- ○ Difference between the gender I feel I am and the sex I was assigned at birth
- ○ Wanting to remove or change my body parts
- ○ Wanting to have the body parts of another gender
- ○ Wanting to be a different gender than the sex assigned at birth
- ○ Wanting to be treated as a different gender
- ○ Feeling or reacting that is typical for a different gender

Did the feeling have a negative impact? If so, how did it impact you?

- ○ On my emotional health
- ○ On my friends, family, or social life
- ○ On my work or education
- ○ On my self-care (diet, sleep, hygiene, exercise)
- ○ No negative impact

Write out your thoughts:

Date:_____ Time:_____

Is the feeling good or bad?

How strong is the feeling? (Circle a number)

1 2 3 4 5 6 7 8 9 10

How would you categorize this feeling?
- ○ Difference between the gender I feel I am and the sex I was assigned at birth
- ○ Wanting to remove or change my body parts
- ○ Wanting to have the body parts of another gender
- ○ Wanting to be a different gender than the sex assigned at birth
- ○ Wanting to be treated as a different gender
- ○ Feeling or reacting that is typical for a different gender

Did the feeling have a negative impact? If so, how did it impact you?
- ○ On my emotional health
- ○ On my friends, family, or social life
- ○ On my work or education
- ○ On my self-care (diet, sleep, hygiene, exercise)
- ○ No negative impact

Write out your thoughts:

Date:_____ Time:_____

Is the feeling good or bad?

How strong is the feeling? (Circle a number)

1   2   3   4   5   6   7   8   9   10

How would you categorize this feeling?
- ○ Difference between the gender I feel I am and the sex I was assigned at birth
- ○ Wanting to remove or change my body parts
- ○ Wanting to have the body parts of another gender
- ○ Wanting to be a different gender than the sex assigned at birth
- ○ Wanting to be treated as a different gender
- ○ Feeling or reacting that is typical for a different gender

Did the feeling have a negative impact? If so, how did it impact you?
- ○ On my emotional health
- ○ On my friends, family, or social life
- ○ On my work or education
- ○ On my self-care (diet, sleep, hygiene, exercise)
- ○ No negative impact

Write out your thoughts:

Date:_____ Time:_____

Is the feeling good or bad?

How strong is the feeling? (Circle a number)

1   2   3   4   5   6   7   8   9   10

How would you categorize this feeling?

- ○ Difference between the gender I feel I am and the sex I was assigned at birth
- ○ Wanting to remove or change my body parts
- ○ Wanting to have the body parts of another gender
- ○ Wanting to be a different gender than the sex assigned at birth
- ○ Wanting to be treated as a different gender
- ○ Feeling or reacting that is typical for a different gender

Did the feeling have a negative impact? If so, how did it impact you?

- ○ On my emotional health
- ○ On my friends, family, or social life
- ○ On my work or education
- ○ On my self-care (diet, sleep, hygiene, exercise)
- ○ No negative impact

Write out your thoughts:

Date:_____ Time:_____

Is the feeling good or bad?

How strong is the feeling? (Circle a number)

1   2   3   4   5   6   7   8   9   10

How would you categorize this feeling?
- ○ Difference between the gender I feel I am and the sex I was assigned at birth
- ○ Wanting to remove or change my body parts
- ○ Wanting to have the body parts of another gender
- ○ Wanting to be a different gender than the sex assigned at birth
- ○ Wanting to be treated as a different gender
- ○ Feeling or reacting that is typical for a different gender

Did the feeling have a negative impact? If so, how did it impact you?
- ○ On my emotional health
- ○ On my friends, family, or social life
- ○ On my work or education
- ○ On my self-care (diet, sleep, hygiene, exercise)
- ○ No negative impact

Write out your thoughts:

Date:_____   Time:_____

Is the feeling good or bad?

How strong is the feeling? (Circle a number)

1   2   3   4   5   6   7   8   9   10

How would you categorize this feeling?
- Difference between the gender I feel I am and the sex I was assigned at birth
- Wanting to remove or change my body parts
- Wanting to have the body parts of another gender
- Wanting to be a different gender than the sex assigned at birth
- Wanting to be treated as a different gender
- Feeling or reacting that is typical for a different gender

Did the feeling have a negative impact? If so, how did it impact you?
- On my emotional health
- On my friends, family, or social life
- On my work or education
- On my self-care (diet, sleep, hygiene, exercise)
- No negative impact

Write out your thoughts:

Date:_____ Time:_____

Is the feeling good or bad?

How strong is the feeling? (Circle a number)

1   2   3   4   5   6   7   8   9   10

How would you categorize this feeling?
- Difference between the gender I feel I am and the sex I was assigned at birth
- Wanting to remove or change my body parts
- Wanting to have the body parts of another gender
- Wanting to be a different gender than the sex assigned at birth
- Wanting to be treated as a different gender
- Feeling or reacting that is typical for a different gender

Did the feeling have a negative impact? If so, how did it impact you?
- On my emotional health
- On my friends, family, or social life
- On my work or education
- On my self-care (diet, sleep, hygiene, exercise)
- No negative impact

Write out your thoughts:

Date:_____ Time:_____

Is the feeling good or bad?

How strong is the feeling? (Circle a number)

1 2 3 4 5 6 7 8 9 10

How would you categorize this feeling?
- Difference between the gender I feel I am and the sex I was assigned at birth
- Wanting to remove or change my body parts
- Wanting to have the body parts of another gender
- Wanting to be a different gender than the sex assigned at birth
- Wanting to be treated as a different gender
- Feeling or reacting that is typical for a different gender

Did the feeling have a negative impact? If so, how did it impact you?
- On my emotional health
- On my friends, family, or social life
- On my work or education
- On my self-care (diet, sleep, hygiene, exercise)
- No negative impact

Write out your thoughts:

Date:_____   Time:_____

Is the feeling good or bad?

How strong is the feeling? (Circle a number)

1   2   3   4   5   6   7   8   9   10

How would you categorize this feeling?
- Difference between the gender I feel I am and the sex I was assigned at birth
- Wanting to remove or change my body parts
- Wanting to have the body parts of another gender
- Wanting to be a different gender than the sex assigned at birth
- Wanting to be treated as a different gender
- Feeling or reacting that is typical for a different gender

Did the feeling have a negative impact? If so, how did it impact you?
- On my emotional health
- On my friends, family, or social life
- On my work or education
- On my self-care (diet, sleep, hygiene, exercise)
- No negative impact

Write out your thoughts:

Date:_____ Time:_____

Is the feeling good or bad?

How strong is the feeling? (Circle a number)

1 2 3 4 5 6 7 8 9 10

How would you categorize this feeling?
- Difference between the gender I feel I am and the sex I was assigned at birth
- Wanting to remove or change my body parts
- Wanting to have the body parts of another gender
- Wanting to be a different gender than the sex assigned at birth
- Wanting to be treated as a different gender
- Feeling or reacting that is typical for a different gender

Did the feeling have a negative impact? If so, how did it impact you?
- On my emotional health
- On my friends, family, or social life
- On my work or education
- On my self-care (diet, sleep, hygiene, exercise)
- No negative impact

Write out your thoughts:

Date:_____ Time:_____

Is the feeling good or bad?

How strong is the feeling? (Circle a number)

1   2   3   4   5   6   7   8   9   10

How would you categorize this feeling?
- Difference between the gender I feel I am and the sex I was assigned at birth
- Wanting to remove or change my body parts
- Wanting to have the body parts of another gender
- Wanting to be a different gender than the sex assigned at birth
- Wanting to be treated as a different gender
- Feeling or reacting that is typical for a different gender

Did the feeling have a negative impact? If so, how did it impact you?
- On my emotional health
- On my friends, family, or social life
- On my work or education
- On my self-care (diet, sleep, hygiene, exercise)
- No negative impact

Write out your thoughts:

Date:_____ Time:_____

Is the feeling good or bad?

How strong is the feeling? (Circle a number)

1 2 3 4 5 6 7 8 9 10

How would you categorize this feeling?
- ○ Difference between the gender I feel I am and the sex I was assigned at birth
- ○ Wanting to remove or change my body parts
- ○ Wanting to have the body parts of another gender
- ○ Wanting to be a different gender than the sex assigned at birth
- ○ Wanting to be treated as a different gender
- ○ Feeling or reacting that is typical for a different gender

Did the feeling have a negative impact? If so, how did it impact you?
- ○ On my emotional health
- ○ On my friends, family, or social life
- ○ On my work or education
- ○ On my self-care (diet, sleep, hygiene, exercise)
- ○ No negative impact

Write out your thoughts:

Date:_____ **Time:**_____

Is the feeling good or bad?

How strong is the feeling? (Circle a number)

1   2   3   4   5   6   7   8   9   10

How would you categorize this feeling?
- Difference between the gender I feel I am and the sex I was assigned at birth
- Wanting to remove or change my body parts
- Wanting to have the body parts of another gender
- Wanting to be a different gender than the sex assigned at birth
- Wanting to be treated as a different gender
- Feeling or reacting that is typical for a different gender

Did the feeling have a negative impact? If so, how did it impact you?
- On my emotional health
- On my friends, family, or social life
- On my work or education
- On my self-care (diet, sleep, hygiene, exercise)
- No negative impact

Write out your thoughts:

Date:_____ Time:_____

Is the feeling good or bad?

How strong is the feeling? (Circle a number)

1   2   3   4   5   6   7   8   9   10

How would you categorize this feeling?
- ○ Difference between the gender I feel I am and the sex I was assigned at birth
- ○ Wanting to remove or change my body parts
- ○ Wanting to have the body parts of another gender
- ○ Wanting to be a different gender than the sex assigned at birth
- ○ Wanting to be treated as a different gender
- ○ Feeling or reacting that is typical for a different gender

Did the feeling have a negative impact? If so, how did it impact you?
- ○ On my emotional health
- ○ On my friends, family, or social life
- ○ On my work or education
- ○ On my self-care (diet, sleep, hygiene, exercise)
- ○ No negative impact

Write out your thoughts:

Date:_____ Time:_____

Is the feeling good or bad?

How strong is the feeling? (Circle a number)

1 2 3 4 5 6 7 8 9 10

How would you categorize this feeling?
- Difference between the gender I feel I am and the sex I was assigned at birth
- Wanting to remove or change my body parts
- Wanting to have the body parts of another gender
- Wanting to be a different gender than the sex assigned at birth
- Wanting to be treated as a different gender
- Feeling or reacting that is typical for a different gender

Did the feeling have a negative impact? If so, how did it impact you?
- On my emotional health
- On my friends, family, or social life
- On my work or education
- On my self-care (diet, sleep, hygiene, exercise)
- No negative impact

Write out your thoughts:

Date:_____ Time:_____

Is the feeling good or bad?

How strong is the feeling? (Circle a number)

1 2 3 4 5 6 7 8 9 10

How would you categorize this feeling?
- Difference between the gender I feel I am and the sex I was assigned at birth
- Wanting to remove or change my body parts
- Wanting to have the body parts of another gender
- Wanting to be a different gender than the sex assigned at birth
- Wanting to be treated as a different gender
- Feeling or reacting that is typical for a different gender

Did the feeling have a negative impact? If so, how did it impact you?
- On my emotional health
- On my friends, family, or social life
- On my work or education
- On my self-care (diet, sleep, hygiene, exercise)
- No negative impact

Write out your thoughts:

Date:_____ Time:_____

Is the feeling good or bad?

How strong is the feeling? (Circle a number)

1   2   3   4   5   6   7   8   9   10

How would you categorize this feeling?
- ○ Difference between the gender I feel I am and the sex I was assigned at birth
- ○ Wanting to remove or change my body parts
- ○ Wanting to have the body parts of another gender
- ○ Wanting to be a different gender than the sex assigned at birth
- ○ Wanting to be treated as a different gender
- ○ Feeling or reacting that is typical for a different gender

Did the feeling have a negative impact? If so, how did it impact you?
- ○ On my emotional health
- ○ On my friends, family, or social life
- ○ On my work or education
- ○ On my self-care (diet, sleep, hygiene, exercise)
- ○ No negative impact

Write out your thoughts:

Date:_____ Time:_____

Is the feeling good or bad?

How strong is the feeling? (Circle a number)

1   2   3   4   5   6   7   8   9   10

How would you categorize this feeling?
- Difference between the gender I feel I am and the sex I was assigned at birth
- Wanting to remove or change my body parts
- Wanting to have the body parts of another gender
- Wanting to be a different gender than the sex assigned at birth
- Wanting to be treated as a different gender
- Feeling or reacting that is typical for a different gender

Did the feeling have a negative impact? If so, how did it impact you?
- On my emotional health
- On my friends, family, or social life
- On my work or education
- On my self-care (diet, sleep, hygiene, exercise)
- No negative impact

Write out your thoughts:

Date:_____ Time:_____

Is the feeling good or bad?

How strong is the feeling? (Circle a number)

1   2   3   4   5   6   7   8   9   10

How would you categorize this feeling?
- ○ Difference between the gender I feel I am and the sex I was assigned at birth
- ○ Wanting to remove or change my body parts
- ○ Wanting to have the body parts of another gender
- ○ Wanting to be a different gender than the sex assigned at birth
- ○ Wanting to be treated as a different gender
- ○ Feeling or reacting that is typical for a different gender

Did the feeling have a negative impact? If so, how did it impact you?
- ○ On my emotional health
- ○ On my friends, family, or social life
- ○ On my work or education
- ○ On my self-care (diet, sleep, hygiene, exercise)
- ○ No negative impact

Write out your thoughts:

Date:_____ **Time:**_____

Is the feeling good or bad?

How strong is the feeling? (Circle a number)

1   2   3   4   5   6   7   8   9   10

How would you categorize this feeling?
- Difference between the gender I feel I am and the sex I was assigned at birth
- Wanting to remove or change my body parts
- Wanting to have the body parts of another gender
- Wanting to be a different gender than the sex assigned at birth
- Wanting to be treated as a different gender
- Feeling or reacting that is typical for a different gender

Did the feeling have a negative impact? If so, how did it impact you?
- On my emotional health
- On my friends, family, or social life
- On my work or education
- On my self-care (diet, sleep, hygiene, exercise)
- No negative impact

Write out your thoughts:

Date:_____ Time:_____

Is the feeling good or bad?

How strong is the feeling? (Circle a number)

1   2   3   4   5   6   7   8   9   10

How would you categorize this feeling?

- ○ Difference between the gender I feel I am and the sex I was assigned at birth
- ○ Wanting to remove or change my body parts
- ○ Wanting to have the body parts of another gender
- ○ Wanting to be a different gender than the sex assigned at birth
- ○ Wanting to be treated as a different gender
- ○ Feeling or reacting that is typical for a different gender

Did the feeling have a negative impact? If so, how did it impact you?

- ○ On my emotional health
- ○ On my friends, family, or social life
- ○ On my work or education
- ○ On my self-care (diet, sleep, hygiene, exercise)
- ○ No negative impact

Write out your thoughts:

Date:_____ **Time:**_____

Is the feeling good or bad?

How strong is the feeling? (Circle a number)
1   2   3   4   5   6   7   8   9   10

How would you categorize this feeling?
- ○ Difference between the gender I feel I am and the sex I was assigned at birth
- ○ Wanting to remove or change my body parts
- ○ Wanting to have the body parts of another gender
- ○ Wanting to be a different gender than the sex assigned at birth
- ○ Wanting to be treated as a different gender
- ○ Feeling or reacting that is typical for a different gender

Did the feeling have a negative impact? If so, how did it impact you?
- ○ On my emotional health
- ○ On my friends, family, or social life
- ○ On my work or education
- ○ On my self-care (diet, sleep, hygiene, exercise)
- ○ No negative impact

Write out your thoughts:

Date:_____ Time:_____

Is the feeling good or bad?

How strong is the feeling? (Circle a number)

1   2   3   4   5   6   7   8   9   10

How would you categorize this feeling?

- Difference between the gender I feel I am and the sex I was assigned at birth
- Wanting to remove or change my body parts
- Wanting to have the body parts of another gender
- Wanting to be a different gender than the sex assigned at birth
- Wanting to be treated as a different gender
- Feeling or reacting that is typical for a different gender

Did the feeling have a negative impact? If so, how did it impact you?

- On my emotional health
- On my friends, family, or social life
- On my work or education
- On my self-care (diet, sleep, hygiene, exercise)
- No negative impact

Write out your thoughts:

Date:_____ Time:_____

Is the feeling good or bad?

How strong is the feeling? (Circle a number)

1 2 3 4 5 6 7 8 9 10

How would you categorize this feeling?
- Difference between the gender I feel I am and the sex I was assigned at birth
- Wanting to remove or change my body parts
- Wanting to have the body parts of another gender
- Wanting to be a different gender than the sex assigned at birth
- Wanting to be treated as a different gender
- Feeling or reacting that is typical for a different gender

Did the feeling have a negative impact? If so, how did it impact you?
- On my emotional health
- On my friends, family, or social life
- On my work or education
- On my self-care (diet, sleep, hygiene, exercise)
- No negative impact

Write out your thoughts:

Date:_____ Time:_____

Is the feeling good or bad?

How strong is the feeling? (Circle a number)

1 2 3 4 5 6 7 8 9 10

How would you categorize this feeling?
- ○ Difference between the gender I feel I am and the sex I was assigned at birth
- ○ Wanting to remove or change my body parts
- ○ Wanting to have the body parts of another gender
- ○ Wanting to be a different gender than the sex assigned at birth
- ○ Wanting to be treated as a different gender
- ○ Feeling or reacting that is typical for a different gender

Did the feeling have a negative impact? If so, how did it impact you?
- ○ On my emotional health
- ○ On my friends, family, or social life
- ○ On my work or education
- ○ On my self-care (diet, sleep, hygiene, exercise)
- ○ No negative impact

Write out your thoughts:

Date:_____ Time:_____

Is the feeling good or bad?

How strong is the feeling? (Circle a number)

1 2 3 4 5 6 7 8 9 10

How would you categorize this feeling?
- ○ Difference between the gender I feel I am and the sex I was assigned at birth
- ○ Wanting to remove or change my body parts
- ○ Wanting to have the body parts of another gender
- ○ Wanting to be a different gender than the sex assigned at birth
- ○ Wanting to be treated as a different gender
- ○ Feeling or reacting that is typical for a different gender

Did the feeling have a negative impact? If so, how did it impact you?
- ○ On my emotional health
- ○ On my friends, family, or social life
- ○ On my work or education
- ○ On my self-care (diet, sleep, hygiene, exercise)
- ○ No negative impact

Write out your thoughts:

Date:_____ Time:_____

Is the feeling good or bad?

How strong is the feeling? (Circle a number)

1   2   3   4   5   6   7   8   9   10

How would you categorize this feeling?
- ○ Difference between the gender I feel I am and the sex I was assigned at birth
- ○ Wanting to remove or change my body parts
- ○ Wanting to have the body parts of another gender
- ○ Wanting to be a different gender than the sex assigned at birth
- ○ Wanting to be treated as a different gender
- ○ Feeling or reacting that is typical for a different gender

Did the feeling have a negative impact? If so, how did it impact you?
- ○ On my emotional health
- ○ On my friends, family, or social life
- ○ On my work or education
- ○ On my self-care (diet, sleep, hygiene, exercise)
- ○ No negative impact

Write out your thoughts:

Date:_____ Time:_____

Is the feeling good or bad?

How strong is the feeling? (Circle a number)

1   2   3   4   5   6   7   8   9   10

How would you categorize this feeling?
- Difference between the gender I feel I am and the sex I was assigned at birth
- Wanting to remove or change my body parts
- Wanting to have the body parts of another gender
- Wanting to be a different gender than the sex assigned at birth
- Wanting to be treated as a different gender
- Feeling or reacting that is typical for a different gender

Did the feeling have a negative impact? If so, how did it impact you?
- On my emotional health
- On my friends, family, or social life
- On my work or education
- On my self-care (diet, sleep, hygiene, exercise)
- No negative impact

Write out your thoughts:

Date:_____ Time:_____

Is the feeling good or bad?

How strong is the feeling? (Circle a number)

1 2 3 4 5 6 7 8 9 10

How would you categorize this feeling?

- ○ Difference between the gender I feel I am and the sex I was assigned at birth
- ○ Wanting to remove or change my body parts
- ○ Wanting to have the body parts of another gender
- ○ Wanting to be a different gender than the sex assigned at birth
- ○ Wanting to be treated as a different gender
- ○ Feeling or reacting that is typical for a different gender

Did the feeling have a negative impact? If so, how did it impact you?

- ○ On my emotional health
- ○ On my friends, family, or social life
- ○ On my work or education
- ○ On my self-care (diet, sleep, hygiene, exercise)
- ○ No negative impact

Write out your thoughts:

Date:_____   Time:_____

Is the feeling good or bad?

How strong is the feeling? (Circle a number)

1 2 3 4 5 6 7 8 9 10

How would you categorize this feeling?
- Difference between the gender I feel I am and the sex I was assigned at birth
- Wanting to remove or change my body parts
- Wanting to have the body parts of another gender
- Wanting to be a different gender than the sex assigned at birth
- Wanting to be treated as a different gender
- Feeling or reacting that is typical for a different gender

Did the feeling have a negative impact? If so, how did it impact you?
- On my emotional health
- On my friends, family, or social life
- On my work or education
- On my self-care (diet, sleep, hygiene, exercise)
- No negative impact

Write out your thoughts:

Date:_____ Time:_____

Is the feeling good or bad?

How strong is the feeling? (Circle a number)

1   2   3   4   5   6   7   8   9   10

How would you categorize this feeling?
- Difference between the gender I feel I am and the sex I was assigned at birth
- Wanting to remove or change my body parts
- Wanting to have the body parts of another gender
- Wanting to be a different gender than the sex assigned at birth
- Wanting to be treated as a different gender
- Feeling or reacting that is typical for a different gender

Did the feeling have a negative impact? If so, how did it impact you?
- On my emotional health
- On my friends, family, or social life
- On my work or education
- On my self-care (diet, sleep, hygiene, exercise)
- No negative impact

Write out your thoughts:

Date:_____ Time:_____

Is the feeling good or bad?

How strong is the feeling? (Circle a number)

1   2   3   4   5   6   7   8   9   10

How would you categorize this feeling?
- Difference between the gender I feel I am and the sex I was assigned at birth
- Wanting to remove or change my body parts
- Wanting to have the body parts of another gender
- Wanting to be a different gender than the sex assigned at birth
- Wanting to be treated as a different gender
- Feeling or reacting that is typical for a different gender

Did the feeling have a negative impact? If so, how did it impact you?
- On my emotional health
- On my friends, family, or social life
- On my work or education
- On my self-care (diet, sleep, hygiene, exercise)
- No negative impact

Write out your thoughts:

Date:_____ Time:_____

Is the feeling good or bad?

How strong is the feeling? (Circle a number)

1   2   3   4   5   6   7   8   9   10

How would you categorize this feeling?
- ○ Difference between the gender I feel I am and the sex I was assigned at birth
- ○ Wanting to remove or change my body parts
- ○ Wanting to have the body parts of another gender
- ○ Wanting to be a different gender than the sex assigned at birth
- ○ Wanting to be treated as a different gender
- ○ Feeling or reacting that is typical for a different gender

Did the feeling have a negative impact? If so, how did it impact you?
- ○ On my emotional health
- ○ On my friends, family, or social life
- ○ On my work or education
- ○ On my self-care (diet, sleep, hygiene, exercise)
- ○ No negative impact

Write out your thoughts:

Date:_____ Time:_____

Is the feeling good or bad?

How strong is the feeling? (Circle a number)

1 2 3 4 5 6 7 8 9 10

How would you categorize this feeling?
- ○ Difference between the gender I feel I am and the sex I was assigned at birth
- ○ Wanting to remove or change my body parts
- ○ Wanting to have the body parts of another gender
- ○ Wanting to be a different gender than the sex assigned at birth
- ○ Wanting to be treated as a different gender
- ○ Feeling or reacting that is typical for a different gender

Did the feeling have a negative impact? If so, how did it impact you?
- ○ On my emotional health
- ○ On my friends, family, or social life
- ○ On my work or education
- ○ On my self-care (diet, sleep, hygiene, exercise)
- ○ No negative impact

Write out your thoughts:

Date:_____ Time:_____

Is the feeling good or bad?

How strong is the feeling? (Circle a number)

1   2   3   4   5   6   7   8   9   10

How would you categorize this feeling?
- Difference between the gender I feel I am and the sex I was assigned at birth
- Wanting to remove or change my body parts
- Wanting to have the body parts of another gender
- Wanting to be a different gender than the sex assigned at birth
- Wanting to be treated as a different gender
- Feeling or reacting that is typical for a different gender

Did the feeling have a negative impact? If so, how did it impact you?
- On my emotional health
- On my friends, family, or social life
- On my work or education
- On my self-care (diet, sleep, hygiene, exercise)
- No negative impact

Write out your thoughts:

Date:_____ Time:_____

Is the feeling good or bad?

How strong is the feeling? (Circle a number)

1   2   3   4   5   6   7   8   9   10

How would you categorize this feeling?
- Difference between the gender I feel I am and the sex I was assigned at birth
- Wanting to remove or change my body parts
- Wanting to have the body parts of another gender
- Wanting to be a different gender than the sex assigned at birth
- Wanting to be treated as a different gender
- Feeling or reacting that is typical for a different gender

Did the feeling have a negative impact? If so, how did it impact you?
- On my emotional health
- On my friends, family, or social life
- On my work or education
- On my self-care (diet, sleep, hygiene, exercise)
- No negative impact

Write out your thoughts:

Date:_____ Time:_____

Is the feeling good or bad?

How strong is the feeling? (Circle a number)
1   2   3   4   5   6   7   8   9   10

How would you categorize this feeling?
○ Difference between the gender I feel I am and the sex I was assigned at birth
○ Wanting to remove or change my body parts
○ Wanting to have the body parts of another gender
○ Wanting to be a different gender than the sex assigned at birth
○ Wanting to be treated as a different gender
○ Feeling or reacting that is typical for a different gender

Did the feeling have a negative impact? If so, how did it impact you?
○ On my emotional health
○ On my friends, family, or social life
○ On my work or education
○ On my self-care (diet, sleep, hygiene, exercise)
○ No negative impact

Write out your thoughts:

Date:_____ Time:_____

Is the feeling good or bad?

How strong is the feeling? (Circle a number)

1   2   3   4   5   6   7   8   9   10

How would you categorize this feeling?
- Difference between the gender I feel I am and the sex I was assigned at birth
- Wanting to remove or change my body parts
- Wanting to have the body parts of another gender
- Wanting to be a different gender than the sex assigned at birth
- Wanting to be treated as a different gender
- Feeling or reacting that is typical for a different gender

Did the feeling have a negative impact? If so, how did it impact you?
- On my emotional health
- On my friends, family, or social life
- On my work or education
- On my self-care (diet, sleep, hygiene, exercise)
- No negative impact

Write out your thoughts:

Date:_____ Time:_____

Is the feeling good or bad?

How strong is the feeling? (Circle a number)

1   2   3   4   5   6   7   8   9   10

How would you categorize this feeling?
- Difference between the gender I feel I am and the sex I was assigned at birth
- Wanting to remove or change my body parts
- Wanting to have the body parts of another gender
- Wanting to be a different gender than the sex assigned at birth
- Wanting to be treated as a different gender
- Feeling or reacting that is typical for a different gender

Did the feeling have a negative impact? If so, how did it impact you?
- On my emotional health
- On my friends, family, or social life
- On my work or education
- On my self-care (diet, sleep, hygiene, exercise)
- No negative impact

Write out your thoughts:

Date:_____ Time:_____

Is the feeling good or bad?

How strong is the feeling? (Circle a number)

1 2 3 4 5 6 7 8 9 10

How would you categorize this feeling?

- ○ Difference between the gender I feel I am and the sex I was assigned at birth
- ○ Wanting to remove or change my body parts
- ○ Wanting to have the body parts of another gender
- ○ Wanting to be a different gender than the sex assigned at birth
- ○ Wanting to be treated as a different gender
- ○ Feeling or reacting that is typical for a different gender

Did the feeling have a negative impact? If so, how did it impact you?

- ○ On my emotional health
- ○ On my friends, family, or social life
- ○ On my work or education
- ○ On my self-care (diet, sleep, hygiene, exercise)
- ○ No negative impact

Write out your thoughts:

Date:_____ Time:_____

Is the feeling good or bad?

How strong is the feeling? (Circle a number)

1 2 3 4 5 6 7 8 9 10

How would you categorize this feeling?

- Difference between the gender I feel I am and the sex I was assigned at birth
- Wanting to remove or change my body parts
- Wanting to have the body parts of another gender
- Wanting to be a different gender than the sex assigned at birth
- Wanting to be treated as a different gender
- Feeling or reacting that is typical for a different gender

Did the feeling have a negative impact? If so, how did it impact you?

- On my emotional health
- On my friends, family, or social life
- On my work or education
- On my self-care (diet, sleep, hygiene, exercise)
- No negative impact

Write out your thoughts:

Date:_____   Time:_____

Is the feeling good or bad?

How strong is the feeling? (Circle a number)

1   2   3   4   5   6   7   8   9   10

How would you categorize this feeling?

- ○ Difference between the gender I feel I am and the sex I was assigned at birth
- ○ Wanting to remove or change my body parts
- ○ Wanting to have the body parts of another gender
- ○ Wanting to be a different gender than the sex assigned at birth
- ○ Wanting to be treated as a different gender
- ○ Feeling or reacting that is typical for a different gender

Did the feeling have a negative impact? If so, how did it impact you?

- ○ On my emotional health
- ○ On my friends, family, or social life
- ○ On my work or education
- ○ On my self-care (diet, sleep, hygiene, exercise)
- ○ No negative impact

Write out your thoughts:

Date:_____ Time:_____

Is the feeling good or bad?

How strong is the feeling? (Circle a number)

1   2   3   4   5   6   7   8   9   10

How would you categorize this feeling?
- ○ Difference between the gender I feel I am and the sex I was assigned at birth
- ○ Wanting to remove or change my body parts
- ○ Wanting to have the body parts of another gender
- ○ Wanting to be a different gender than the sex assigned at birth
- ○ Wanting to be treated as a different gender
- ○ Feeling or reacting that is typical for a different gender

Did the feeling have a negative impact? If so, how did it impact you?
- ○ On my emotional health
- ○ On my friends, family, or social life
- ○ On my work or education
- ○ On my self-care (diet, sleep, hygiene, exercise)
- ○ No negative impact

Write out your thoughts:

Date:_____ Time:_____

Is the feeling good or bad?

How strong is the feeling? (Circle a number)

1   2   3   4   5   6   7   8   9   10

How would you categorize this feeling?

- Difference between the gender I feel I am and the sex I was assigned at birth
- Wanting to remove or change my body parts
- Wanting to have the body parts of another gender
- Wanting to be a different gender than the sex assigned at birth
- Wanting to be treated as a different gender
- Feeling or reacting that is typical for a different gender

Did the feeling have a negative impact? If so, how did it impact you?

- On my emotional health
- On my friends, family, or social life
- On my work or education
- On my self-care (diet, sleep, hygiene, exercise)
- No negative impact

Write out your thoughts:

Date:_____ Time:_____

Is the feeling good or bad?

How strong is the feeling? (Circle a number)

1 2 3 4 5 6 7 8 9 10

How would you categorize this feeling?
- ○ Difference between the gender I feel I am and the sex I was assigned at birth
- ○ Wanting to remove or change my body parts
- ○ Wanting to have the body parts of another gender
- ○ Wanting to be a different gender than the sex assigned at birth
- ○ Wanting to be treated as a different gender
- ○ Feeling or reacting that is typical for a different gender

Did the feeling have a negative impact? If so, how did it impact you?
- ○ On my emotional health
- ○ On my friends, family, or social life
- ○ On my work or education
- ○ On my self-care (diet, sleep, hygiene, exercise)
- ○ No negative impact

Write out your thoughts:

Date:_____ **Time:**_____

Is the feeling good or bad?

How strong is the feeling? (Circle a number)

1   2   3   4   5   6   7   8   9   10

How would you categorize this feeling?
- Difference between the gender I feel I am and the sex I was assigned at birth
- Wanting to remove or change my body parts
- Wanting to have the body parts of another gender
- Wanting to be a different gender than the sex assigned at birth
- Wanting to be treated as a different gender
- Feeling or reacting that is typical for a different gender

Did the feeling have a negative impact? If so, how did it impact you?
- On my emotional health
- On my friends, family, or social life
- On my work or education
- On my self-care (diet, sleep, hygiene, exercise)
- No negative impact

Write out your thoughts:

Date:_____ Time:_____

Is the feeling good or bad?

How strong is the feeling? (Circle a number)

1   2   3   4   5   6   7   8   9   10

How would you categorize this feeling?
- Difference between the gender I feel I am and the sex I was assigned at birth
- Wanting to remove or change my body parts
- Wanting to have the body parts of another gender
- Wanting to be a different gender than the sex assigned at birth
- Wanting to be treated as a different gender
- Feeling or reacting that is typical for a different gender

Did the feeling have a negative impact? If so, how did it impact you?
- On my emotional health
- On my friends, family, or social life
- On my work or education
- On my self-care (diet, sleep, hygiene, exercise)
- No negative impact

Write out your thoughts:

Date:_____ Time:_____

Is the feeling good or bad?

How strong is the feeling? (Circle a number)

1   2   3   4   5   6   7   8   9   10

How would you categorize this feeling?
- Difference between the gender I feel I am and the sex I was assigned at birth
- Wanting to remove or change my body parts
- Wanting to have the body parts of another gender
- Wanting to be a different gender than the sex assigned at birth
- Wanting to be treated as a different gender
- Feeling or reacting that is typical for a different gender

Did the feeling have a negative impact? If so, how did it impact you?
- On my emotional health
- On my friends, family, or social life
- On my work or education
- On my self-care (diet, sleep, hygiene, exercise)
- No negative impact

Write out your thoughts:

Date:_____   Time:_____

Is the feeling good or bad?

How strong is the feeling? (Circle a number)

1   2   3   4   5   6   7   8   9   10

How would you categorize this feeling?
- Difference between the gender I feel I am and the sex I was assigned at birth
- Wanting to remove or change my body parts
- Wanting to have the body parts of another gender
- Wanting to be a different gender than the sex assigned at birth
- Wanting to be treated as a different gender
- Feeling or reacting that is typical for a different gender

Did the feeling have a negative impact? If so, how did it impact you?
- On my emotional health
- On my friends, family, or social life
- On my work or education
- On my self-care (diet, sleep, hygiene, exercise)
- No negative impact

Write out your thoughts:

Date:_____ Time:_____

Is the feeling good or bad?

How strong is the feeling? (Circle a number)

1 2 3 4 5 6 7 8 9 10

How would you categorize this feeling?
- ○ Difference between the gender I feel I am and the sex I was assigned at birth
- ○ Wanting to remove or change my body parts
- ○ Wanting to have the body parts of another gender
- ○ Wanting to be a different gender than the sex assigned at birth
- ○ Wanting to be treated as a different gender
- ○ Feeling or reacting that is typical for a different gender

Did the feeling have a negative impact? If so, how did it impact you?
- ○ On my emotional health
- ○ On my friends, family, or social life
- ○ On my work or education
- ○ On my self-care (diet, sleep, hygiene, exercise)
- ○ No negative impact

Write out your thoughts:

Date:_____ Time:_____

Is the feeling good or bad?

How strong is the feeling? (Circle a number)

1 2 3 4 5 6 7 8 9 10

How would you categorize this feeling?
- Difference between the gender I feel I am and the sex I was assigned at birth
- Wanting to remove or change my body parts
- Wanting to have the body parts of another gender
- Wanting to be a different gender than the sex assigned at birth
- Wanting to be treated as a different gender
- Feeling or reacting that is typical for a different gender

Did the feeling have a negative impact? If so, how did it impact you?
- On my emotional health
- On my friends, family, or social life
- On my work or education
- On my self-care (diet, sleep, hygiene, exercise)
- No negative impact

Write out your thoughts:

Date:_____ Time:_____

Is the feeling good or bad?

How strong is the feeling? (Circle a number)

1   2   3   4   5   6   7   8   9   10

How would you categorize this feeling?
- Difference between the gender I feel I am and the sex I was assigned at birth
- Wanting to remove or change my body parts
- Wanting to have the body parts of another gender
- Wanting to be a different gender than the sex assigned at birth
- Wanting to be treated as a different gender
- Feeling or reacting that is typical for a different gender

Did the feeling have a negative impact? If so, how did it impact you?
- On my emotional health
- On my friends, family, or social life
- On my work or education
- On my self-care (diet, sleep, hygiene, exercise)
- No negative impact

Write out your thoughts:

Date:_____ Time:_____

Is the feeling good or bad?

How strong is the feeling? (Circle a number)

1   2   3   4   5   6   7   8   9   10

How would you categorize this feeling?
- ○ Difference between the gender I feel I am and the sex I was assigned at birth
- ○ Wanting to remove or change my body parts
- ○ Wanting to have the body parts of another gender
- ○ Wanting to be a different gender than the sex assigned at birth
- ○ Wanting to be treated as a different gender
- ○ Feeling or reacting that is typical for a different gender

Did the feeling have a negative impact? If so, how did it impact you?
- ○ On my emotional health
- ○ On my friends, family, or social life
- ○ On my work or education
- ○ On my self-care (diet, sleep, hygiene, exercise)
- ○ No negative impact

Write out your thoughts:

Date:_____ Time:_____

Is the feeling good or bad?

How strong is the feeling? (Circle a number)

1　2　3　4　5　6　7　8　9　10

How would you categorize this feeling?
- Difference between the gender I feel I am and the sex I was assigned at birth
- Wanting to remove or change my body parts
- Wanting to have the body parts of another gender
- Wanting to be a different gender than the sex assigned at birth
- Wanting to be treated as a different gender
- Feeling or reacting that is typical for a different gender

Did the feeling have a negative impact? If so, how did it impact you?
- On my emotional health
- On my friends, family, or social life
- On my work or education
- On my self-care (diet, sleep, hygiene, exercise)
- No negative impact

Write out your thoughts:

Date:_____ Time:_____

Is the feeling good or bad?

How strong is the feeling? (Circle a number)

1 2 3 4 5 6 7 8 9 10

How would you categorize this feeling?
- ○ Difference between the gender I feel I am and the sex I was assigned at birth
- ○ Wanting to remove or change my body parts
- ○ Wanting to have the body parts of another gender
- ○ Wanting to be a different gender than the sex assigned at birth
- ○ Wanting to be treated as a different gender
- ○ Feeling or reacting that is typical for a different gender

Did the feeling have a negative impact? If so, how did it impact you?
- ○ On my emotional health
- ○ On my friends, family, or social life
- ○ On my work or education
- ○ On my self-care (diet, sleep, hygiene, exercise)
- ○ No negative impact

Write out your thoughts:

Date:_____ Time:_____

Is the feeling good or bad?

How strong is the feeling? (Circle a number)

1   2   3   4   5   6   7   8   9   10

How would you categorize this feeling?
- Difference between the gender I feel I am and the sex I was assigned at birth
- Wanting to remove or change my body parts
- Wanting to have the body parts of another gender
- Wanting to be a different gender than the sex assigned at birth
- Wanting to be treated as a different gender
- Feeling or reacting that is typical for a different gender

Did the feeling have a negative impact? If so, how did it impact you?
- On my emotional health
- On my friends, family, or social life
- On my work or education
- On my self-care (diet, sleep, hygiene, exercise)
- No negative impact

Write out your thoughts:

Date:_____ Time:_____

Is the feeling good or bad?

How strong is the feeling? (Circle a number)

1   2   3   4   5   6   7   8   9   10

How would you categorize this feeling?
- ○ Difference between the gender I feel I am and the sex I was assigned at birth
- ○ Wanting to remove or change my body parts
- ○ Wanting to have the body parts of another gender
- ○ Wanting to be a different gender than the sex assigned at birth
- ○ Wanting to be treated as a different gender
- ○ Feeling or reacting that is typical for a different gender

Did the feeling have a negative impact? If so, how did it impact you?
- ○ On my emotional health
- ○ On my friends, family, or social life
- ○ On my work or education
- ○ On my self-care (diet, sleep, hygiene, exercise)
- ○ No negative impact

Write out your thoughts:

Date:_____ Time:_____

Is the feeling good or bad?

How strong is the feeling? (Circle a number)

1   2   3   4   5   6   7   8   9   10

How would you categorize this feeling?
- Difference between the gender I feel I am and the sex I was assigned at birth
- Wanting to remove or change my body parts
- Wanting to have the body parts of another gender
- Wanting to be a different gender than the sex assigned at birth
- Wanting to be treated as a different gender
- Feeling or reacting that is typical for a different gender

Did the feeling have a negative impact? If so, how did it impact you?
- On my emotional health
- On my friends, family, or social life
- On my work or education
- On my self-care (diet, sleep, hygiene, exercise)
- No negative impact

Write out your thoughts:

Date:_____   **Time:**_____

Is the feeling good or bad?

How strong is the feeling? (Circle a number)

1   2   3   4   5   6   7   8   9   10

How would you categorize this feeling?
- Difference between the gender I feel I am and the sex I was assigned at birth
- Wanting to remove or change my body parts
- Wanting to have the body parts of another gender
- Wanting to be a different gender than the sex assigned at birth
- Wanting to be treated as a different gender
- Feeling or reacting that is typical for a different gender

Did the feeling have a negative impact? If so, how did it impact you?
- On my emotional health
- On my friends, family, or social life
- On my work or education
- On my self-care (diet, sleep, hygiene, exercise)
- No negative impact

Write out your thoughts:

Date:_____ Time:_____

Is the feeling good or bad?

How strong is the feeling? (Circle a number)

1 2 3 4 5 6 7 8 9 10

How would you categorize this feeling?
- Difference between the gender I feel I am and the sex I was assigned at birth
- Wanting to remove or change my body parts
- Wanting to have the body parts of another gender
- Wanting to be a different gender than the sex assigned at birth
- Wanting to be treated as a different gender
- Feeling or reacting that is typical for a different gender

Did the feeling have a negative impact? If so, how did it impact you?
- On my emotional health
- On my friends, family, or social life
- On my work or education
- On my self-care (diet, sleep, hygiene, exercise)
- No negative impact

Write out your thoughts:

Date:_____ Time:_____

Is the feeling good or bad?

How strong is the feeling? (Circle a number)

1 2 3 4 5 6 7 8 9 10

How would you categorize this feeling?
- Difference between the gender I feel I am and the sex I was assigned at birth
- Wanting to remove or change my body parts
- Wanting to have the body parts of another gender
- Wanting to be a different gender than the sex assigned at birth
- Wanting to be treated as a different gender
- Feeling or reacting that is typical for a different gender

Did the feeling have a negative impact? If so, how did it impact you?
- On my emotional health
- On my friends, family, or social life
- On my work or education
- On my self-care (diet, sleep, hygiene, exercise)
- No negative impact

Write out your thoughts:

Date:_____ Time:_____

Is the feeling good or bad?

How strong is the feeling? (Circle a number)

1 2 3 4 5 6 7 8 9 10

How would you categorize this feeling?
- ○ Difference between the gender I feel I am and the sex I was assigned at birth
- ○ Wanting to remove or change my body parts
- ○ Wanting to have the body parts of another gender
- ○ Wanting to be a different gender than the sex assigned at birth
- ○ Wanting to be treated as a different gender
- ○ Feeling or reacting that is typical for a different gender

Did the feeling have a negative impact? If so, how did it impact you?
- ○ On my emotional health
- ○ On my friends, family, or social life
- ○ On my work or education
- ○ On my self-care (diet, sleep, hygiene, exercise)
- ○ No negative impact

Write out your thoughts:

Date:_____   Time:_____

Is the feeling good or bad?

How strong is the feeling? (Circle a number)

1   2   3   4   5   6   7   8   9   10

How would you categorize this feeling?
- Difference between the gender I feel I am and the sex I was assigned at birth
- Wanting to remove or change my body parts
- Wanting to have the body parts of another gender
- Wanting to be a different gender than the sex assigned at birth
- Wanting to be treated as a different gender
- Feeling or reacting that is typical for a different gender

Did the feeling have a negative impact? If so, how did it impact you?
- On my emotional health
- On my friends, family, or social life
- On my work or education
- On my self-care (diet, sleep, hygiene, exercise)
- No negative impact

Write out your thoughts:

Date:_____ Time:_____

Is the feeling good or bad?

How strong is the feeling? (Circle a number)

1   2   3   4   5   6   7   8   9   10

How would you categorize this feeling?
- Difference between the gender I feel I am and the sex I was assigned at birth
- Wanting to remove or change my body parts
- Wanting to have the body parts of another gender
- Wanting to be a different gender than the sex assigned at birth
- Wanting to be treated as a different gender
- Feeling or reacting that is typical for a different gender

Did the feeling have a negative impact? If so, how did it impact you?
- On my emotional health
- On my friends, family, or social life
- On my work or education
- On my self-care (diet, sleep, hygiene, exercise)
- No negative impact

Write out your thoughts:

Date:_____ Time:_____

Is the feeling good or bad?

How strong is the feeling? (Circle a number)

1   2   3   4   5   6   7   8   9   10

How would you categorize this feeling?
- ○ Difference between the gender I feel I am and the sex I was assigned at birth
- ○ Wanting to remove or change my body parts
- ○ Wanting to have the body parts of another gender
- ○ Wanting to be a different gender than the sex assigned at birth
- ○ Wanting to be treated as a different gender
- ○ Feeling or reacting that is typical for a different gender

Did the feeling have a negative impact? If so, how did it impact you?
- ○ On my emotional health
- ○ On my friends, family, or social life
- ○ On my work or education
- ○ On my self-care (diet, sleep, hygiene, exercise)
- ○ No negative impact

Write out your thoughts:

Date:_____ Time:_____

Is the feeling good or bad?

How strong is the feeling? (Circle a number)

1   2   3   4   5   6   7   8   9   10

How would you categorize this feeling?
- Difference between the gender I feel I am and the sex I was assigned at birth
- Wanting to remove or change my body parts
- Wanting to have the body parts of another gender
- Wanting to be a different gender than the sex assigned at birth
- Wanting to be treated as a different gender
- Feeling or reacting that is typical for a different gender

Did the feeling have a negative impact? If so, how did it impact you?
- On my emotional health
- On my friends, family, or social life
- On my work or education
- On my self-care (diet, sleep, hygiene, exercise)
- No negative impact

Write out your thoughts:

Date:_____ Time:_____

Is the feeling good or bad?

How strong is the feeling? (Circle a number)

1 2 3 4 5 6 7 8 9 10

How would you categorize this feeling?
- Difference between the gender I feel I am and the sex I was assigned at birth
- Wanting to remove or change my body parts
- Wanting to have the body parts of another gender
- Wanting to be a different gender than the sex assigned at birth
- Wanting to be treated as a different gender
- Feeling or reacting that is typical for a different gender

Did the feeling have a negative impact? If so, how did it impact you?
- On my emotional health
- On my friends, family, or social life
- On my work or education
- On my self-care (diet, sleep, hygiene, exercise)
- No negative impact

Write out your thoughts:

Date:_____   Time:_____

Is the feeling good or bad?

How strong is the feeling? (Circle a number)

1   2   3   4   5   6   7   8   9   10

How would you categorize this feeling?
- Difference between the gender I feel I am and the sex I was assigned at birth
- Wanting to remove or change my body parts
- Wanting to have the body parts of another gender
- Wanting to be a different gender than the sex assigned at birth
- Wanting to be treated as a different gender
- Feeling or reacting that is typical for a different gender

Did the feeling have a negative impact? If so, how did it impact you?
- On my emotional health
- On my friends, family, or social life
- On my work or education
- On my self-care (diet, sleep, hygiene, exercise)
- No negative impact

Write out your thoughts:

Date:_____ Time:_____

Is the feeling good or bad?

How strong is the feeling? (Circle a number)

1 2 3 4 5 6 7 8 9 10

How would you categorize this feeling?

- ○ Difference between the gender I feel I am and the sex I was assigned at birth
- ○ Wanting to remove or change my body parts
- ○ Wanting to have the body parts of another gender
- ○ Wanting to be a different gender than the sex assigned at birth
- ○ Wanting to be treated as a different gender
- ○ Feeling or reacting that is typical for a different gender

Did the feeling have a negative impact? If so, how did it impact you?

- ○ On my emotional health
- ○ On my friends, family, or social life
- ○ On my work or education
- ○ On my self-care (diet, sleep, hygiene, exercise)
- ○ No negative impact

Write out your thoughts:

Date:_____ Time:_____

Is the feeling good or bad?

How strong is the feeling? (Circle a number)

1 2 3 4 5 6 7 8 9 10

How would you categorize this feeling?
- Difference between the gender I feel I am and the sex I was assigned at birth
- Wanting to remove or change my body parts
- Wanting to have the body parts of another gender
- Wanting to be a different gender than the sex assigned at birth
- Wanting to be treated as a different gender
- Feeling or reacting that is typical for a different gender

Did the feeling have a negative impact? If so, how did it impact you?
- On my emotional health
- On my friends, family, or social life
- On my work or education
- On my self-care (diet, sleep, hygiene, exercise)
- No negative impact

Write out your thoughts:

Date:_____ Time:_____

Is the feeling good or bad?

How strong is the feeling? (Circle a number)

1   2   3   4   5   6   7   8   9   10

How would you categorize this feeling?

- ○ Difference between the gender I feel I am and the sex I was assigned at birth
- ○ Wanting to remove or change my body parts
- ○ Wanting to have the body parts of another gender
- ○ Wanting to be a different gender than the sex assigned at birth
- ○ Wanting to be treated as a different gender
- ○ Feeling or reacting that is typical for a different gender

Did the feeling have a negative impact? If so, how did it impact you?

- ○ On my emotional health
- ○ On my friends, family, or social life
- ○ On my work or education
- ○ On my self-care (diet, sleep, hygiene, exercise)
- ○ No negative impact

Write out your thoughts:

Date:_____ Time:_____

Is the feeling good or bad?

How strong is the feeling? (Circle a number)

1   2   3   4   5   6   7   8   9   10

How would you categorize this feeling?

- ○ Difference between the gender I feel I am and the sex I was assigned at birth
- ○ Wanting to remove or change my body parts
- ○ Wanting to have the body parts of another gender
- ○ Wanting to be a different gender than the sex assigned at birth
- ○ Wanting to be treated as a different gender
- ○ Feeling or reacting that is typical for a different gender

Did the feeling have a negative impact? If so, how did it impact you?

- ○ On my emotional health
- ○ On my friends, family, or social life
- ○ On my work or education
- ○ On my self-care (diet, sleep, hygiene, exercise)
- ○ No negative impact

Write out your thoughts:

Date:_____ Time:_____

Is the feeling good or bad?

How strong is the feeling? (Circle a number)
1   2   3   4   5   6   7   8   9   10

How would you categorize this feeling?
- Difference between the gender I feel I am and the sex I was assigned at birth
- Wanting to remove or change my body parts
- Wanting to have the body parts of another gender
- Wanting to be a different gender than the sex assigned at birth
- Wanting to be treated as a different gender
- Feeling or reacting that is typical for a different gender

Did the feeling have a negative impact? If so, how did it impact you?
- On my emotional health
- On my friends, family, or social life
- On my work or education
- On my self-care (diet, sleep, hygiene, exercise)
- No negative impact

Write out your thoughts:

Date:_____ Time:_____

Is the feeling good or bad?

How strong is the feeling? (Circle a number)

1   2   3   4   5   6   7   8   9   10

How would you categorize this feeling?

- ○ Difference between the gender I feel I am and the sex I was assigned at birth
- ○ Wanting to remove or change my body parts
- ○ Wanting to have the body parts of another gender
- ○ Wanting to be a different gender than the sex assigned at birth
- ○ Wanting to be treated as a different gender
- ○ Feeling or reacting that is typical for a different gender

Did the feeling have a negative impact? If so, how did it impact you?

- ○ On my emotional health
- ○ On my friends, family, or social life
- ○ On my work or education
- ○ On my self-care (diet, sleep, hygiene, exercise)
- ○ No negative impact

Write out your thoughts:

Date:_____ Time:_____

Is the feeling good or bad?

How strong is the feeling? (Circle a number)

1   2   3   4   5   6   7   8   9   10

How would you categorize this feeling?
- Difference between the gender I feel I am and the sex I was assigned at birth
- Wanting to remove or change my body parts
- Wanting to have the body parts of another gender
- Wanting to be a different gender than the sex assigned at birth
- Wanting to be treated as a different gender
- Feeling or reacting that is typical for a different gender

Did the feeling have a negative impact? If so, how did it impact you?
- On my emotional health
- On my friends, family, or social life
- On my work or education
- On my self-care (diet, sleep, hygiene, exercise)
- No negative impact

Write out your thoughts:

Date:_____ Time:_____

Is the feeling good or bad?

How strong is the feeling? (Circle a number)

1 2 3 4 5 6 7 8 9 10

How would you categorize this feeling?
- Difference between the gender I feel I am and the sex I was assigned at birth
- Wanting to remove or change my body parts
- Wanting to have the body parts of another gender
- Wanting to be a different gender than the sex assigned at birth
- Wanting to be treated as a different gender
- Feeling or reacting that is typical for a different gender

Did the feeling have a negative impact? If so, how did it impact you?
- On my emotional health
- On my friends, family, or social life
- On my work or education
- On my self-care (diet, sleep, hygiene, exercise)
- No negative impact

Write out your thoughts:

Date:_____ **Time:**_____

Is the feeling good or bad?

How strong is the feeling? (Circle a number)

1 2 3 4 5 6 7 8 9 10

How would you categorize this feeling?
- ○ Difference between the gender I feel I am and the sex I was assigned at birth
- ○ Wanting to remove or change my body parts
- ○ Wanting to have the body parts of another gender
- ○ Wanting to be a different gender than the sex assigned at birth
- ○ Wanting to be treated as a different gender
- ○ Feeling or reacting that is typical for a different gender

Did the feeling have a negative impact? If so, how did it impact you?
- ○ On my emotional health
- ○ On my friends, family, or social life
- ○ On my work or education
- ○ On my self-care (diet, sleep, hygiene, exercise)
- ○ No negative impact

Write out your thoughts:

Date:_____ Time:_____

Is the feeling good or bad?

How strong is the feeling? (Circle a number)

1 2 3 4 5 6 7 8 9 10

How would you categorize this feeling?

- ○ Difference between the gender I feel I am and the sex I was assigned at birth
- ○ Wanting to remove or change my body parts
- ○ Wanting to have the body parts of another gender
- ○ Wanting to be a different gender than the sex assigned at birth
- ○ Wanting to be treated as a different gender
- ○ Feeling or reacting that is typical for a different gender

Did the feeling have a negative impact? If so, how did it impact you?

- ○ On my emotional health
- ○ On my friends, family, or social life
- ○ On my work or education
- ○ On my self-care (diet, sleep, hygiene, exercise)
- ○ No negative impact

Write out your thoughts:

Date:_____   Time:_____

Is the feeling good or bad?

How strong is the feeling? (Circle a number)

1   2   3   4   5   6   7   8   9   10

How would you categorize this feeling?
- ○ Difference between the gender I feel I am and the sex I was assigned at birth
- ○ Wanting to remove or change my body parts
- ○ Wanting to have the body parts of another gender
- ○ Wanting to be a different gender than the sex assigned at birth
- ○ Wanting to be treated as a different gender
- ○ Feeling or reacting that is typical for a different gender

Did the feeling have a negative impact? If so, how did it impact you?
- ○ On my emotional health
- ○ On my friends, family, or social life
- ○ On my work or education
- ○ On my self-care (diet, sleep, hygiene, exercise)
- ○ No negative impact

Write out your thoughts:

Date:_____ Time:_____

Is the feeling good or bad?

How strong is the feeling? (Circle a number)

1   2   3   4   5   6   7   8   9   10

How would you categorize this feeling?
- Difference between the gender I feel I am and the sex I was assigned at birth
- Wanting to remove or change my body parts
- Wanting to have the body parts of another gender
- Wanting to be a different gender than the sex assigned at birth
- Wanting to be treated as a different gender
- Feeling or reacting that is typical for a different gender

Did the feeling have a negative impact? If so, how did it impact you?
- On my emotional health
- On my friends, family, or social life
- On my work or education
- On my self-care (diet, sleep, hygiene, exercise)
- No negative impact

Write out your thoughts:

Date:_____ **Time:**_____

Is the feeling good or bad?

How strong is the feeling? (Circle a number)

1 2 3 4 5 6 7 8 9 10

How would you categorize this feeling?
- Difference between the gender I feel I am and the sex I was assigned at birth
- Wanting to remove or change my body parts
- Wanting to have the body parts of another gender
- Wanting to be a different gender than the sex assigned at birth
- Wanting to be treated as a different gender
- Feeling or reacting that is typical for a different gender

Did the feeling have a negative impact? If so, how did it impact you?
- On my emotional health
- On my friends, family, or social life
- On my work or education
- On my self-care (diet, sleep, hygiene, exercise)
- No negative impact

Write out your thoughts:

Date:_____ Time:_____

Is the feeling good or bad?

How strong is the feeling? (Circle a number)

1 2 3 4 5 6 7 8 9 10

How would you categorize this feeling?

- ○ Difference between the gender I feel I am and the sex I was assigned at birth
- ○ Wanting to remove or change my body parts
- ○ Wanting to have the body parts of another gender
- ○ Wanting to be a different gender than the sex assigned at birth
- ○ Wanting to be treated as a different gender
- ○ Feeling or reacting that is typical for a different gender

Did the feeling have a negative impact? If so, how did it impact you?

- ○ On my emotional health
- ○ On my friends, family, or social life
- ○ On my work or education
- ○ On my self-care (diet, sleep, hygiene, exercise)
- ○ No negative impact

Write out your thoughts:

Date:_____ Time:_____

Is the feeling good or bad?

How strong is the feeling? (Circle a number)

1 2 3 4 5 6 7 8 9 10

How would you categorize this feeling?
- Difference between the gender I feel I am and the sex I was assigned at birth
- Wanting to remove or change my body parts
- Wanting to have the body parts of another gender
- Wanting to be a different gender than the sex assigned at birth
- Wanting to be treated as a different gender
- Feeling or reacting that is typical for a different gender

Did the feeling have a negative impact? If so, how did it impact you?
- On my emotional health
- On my friends, family, or social life
- On my work or education
- On my self-care (diet, sleep, hygiene, exercise)
- No negative impact

Write out your thoughts:

Date:_____ Time:_____

Is the feeling good or bad?

How strong is the feeling? (Circle a number)

1   2   3   4   5   6   7   8   9   10

How would you categorize this feeling?
- Difference between the gender I feel I am and the sex I was assigned at birth
- Wanting to remove or change my body parts
- Wanting to have the body parts of another gender
- Wanting to be a different gender than the sex assigned at birth
- Wanting to be treated as a different gender
- Feeling or reacting that is typical for a different gender

Did the feeling have a negative impact? If so, how did it impact you?
- On my emotional health
- On my friends, family, or social life
- On my work or education
- On my self-care (diet, sleep, hygiene, exercise)
- No negative impact

Write out your thoughts:

Date:_____ Time:_____

Is the feeling good or bad?

How strong is the feeling? (Circle a number)

1   2   3   4   5   6   7   8   9   10

How would you categorize this feeling?
- Difference between the gender I feel I am and the sex I was assigned at birth
- Wanting to remove or change my body parts
- Wanting to have the body parts of another gender
- Wanting to be a different gender than the sex assigned at birth
- Wanting to be treated as a different gender
- Feeling or reacting that is typical for a different gender

Did the feeling have a negative impact? If so, how did it impact you?
- On my emotional health
- On my friends, family, or social life
- On my work or education
- On my self-care (diet, sleep, hygiene, exercise)
- No negative impact

Write out your thoughts:

Date:_____ Time:_____

Is the feeling good or bad?

How strong is the feeling? (Circle a number)

1   2   3   4   5   6   7   8   9   10

How would you categorize this feeling?

- ○ Difference between the gender I feel I am and the sex I was assigned at birth
- ○ Wanting to remove or change my body parts
- ○ Wanting to have the body parts of another gender
- ○ Wanting to be a different gender than the sex assigned at birth
- ○ Wanting to be treated as a different gender
- ○ Feeling or reacting that is typical for a different gender

Did the feeling have a negative impact? If so, how did it impact you?

- ○ On my emotional health
- ○ On my friends, family, or social life
- ○ On my work or education
- ○ On my self-care (diet, sleep, hygiene, exercise)
- ○ No negative impact

Write out your thoughts:

Date:_____ **Time:**_____

Is the feeling good or bad?

How strong is the feeling? (Circle a number)

1 2 3 4 5 6 7 8 9 10

How would you categorize this feeling?
- Difference between the gender I feel I am and the sex I was assigned at birth
- Wanting to remove or change my body parts
- Wanting to have the body parts of another gender
- Wanting to be a different gender than the sex assigned at birth
- Wanting to be treated as a different gender
- Feeling or reacting that is typical for a different gender

Did the feeling have a negative impact? If so, how did it impact you?
- On my emotional health
- On my friends, family, or social life
- On my work or education
- On my self-care (diet, sleep, hygiene, exercise)
- No negative impact

Write out your thoughts:

Date:_____ Time:_____

Is the feeling good or bad?

How strong is the feeling? (Circle a number)

1 2 3 4 5 6 7 8 9 10

How would you categorize this feeling?
- Difference between the gender I feel I am and the sex I was assigned at birth
- Wanting to remove or change my body parts
- Wanting to have the body parts of another gender
- Wanting to be a different gender than the sex assigned at birth
- Wanting to be treated as a different gender
- Feeling or reacting that is typical for a different gender

Did the feeling have a negative impact? If so, how did it impact you?
- On my emotional health
- On my friends, family, or social life
- On my work or education
- On my self-care (diet, sleep, hygiene, exercise)
- No negative impact

Write out your thoughts:

Date:_____ Time:_____

Is the feeling good or bad?

How strong is the feeling? (Circle a number)

1   2   3   4   5   6   7   8   9   10

How would you categorize this feeling?
- Difference between the gender I feel I am and the sex I was assigned at birth
- Wanting to remove or change my body parts
- Wanting to have the body parts of another gender
- Wanting to be a different gender than the sex assigned at birth
- Wanting to be treated as a different gender
- Feeling or reacting that is typical for a different gender

Did the feeling have a negative impact? If so, how did it impact you?
- On my emotional health
- On my friends, family, or social life
- On my work or education
- On my self-care (diet, sleep, hygiene, exercise)
- No negative impact

Write out your thoughts:

Date:_____   **Time:**_____

Is the feeling good or bad?

How strong is the feeling? (Circle a number)

1   2   3   4   5   6   7   8   9   10

How would you categorize this feeling?
- Difference between the gender I feel I am and the sex I was assigned at birth
- Wanting to remove or change my body parts
- Wanting to have the body parts of another gender
- Wanting to be a different gender than the sex assigned at birth
- Wanting to be treated as a different gender
- Feeling or reacting that is typical for a different gender

Did the feeling have a negative impact? If so, how did it impact you?
- On my emotional health
- On my friends, family, or social life
- On my work or education
- On my self-care (diet, sleep, hygiene, exercise)
- No negative impact

Write out your thoughts:

Date:_____ Time:_____

Is the feeling good or bad?

How strong is the feeling? (Circle a number)

1 2 3 4 5 6 7 8 9 10

How would you categorize this feeling?
- Difference between the gender I feel I am and the sex I was assigned at birth
- Wanting to remove or change my body parts
- Wanting to have the body parts of another gender
- Wanting to be a different gender than the sex assigned at birth
- Wanting to be treated as a different gender
- Feeling or reacting that is typical for a different gender

Did the feeling have a negative impact? If so, how did it impact you?
- On my emotional health
- On my friends, family, or social life
- On my work or education
- On my self-care (diet, sleep, hygiene, exercise)
- No negative impact

Write out your thoughts:

Date:_____ Time:_____

Is the feeling good or bad?

How strong is the feeling? (Circle a number)

1 2 3 4 5 6 7 8 9 10

How would you categorize this feeling?
- Difference between the gender I feel I am and the sex I was assigned at birth
- Wanting to remove or change my body parts
- Wanting to have the body parts of another gender
- Wanting to be a different gender than the sex assigned at birth
- Wanting to be treated as a different gender
- Feeling or reacting that is typical for a different gender

Did the feeling have a negative impact? If so, how did it impact you?
- On my emotional health
- On my friends, family, or social life
- On my work or education
- On my self-care (diet, sleep, hygiene, exercise)
- No negative impact

Write out your thoughts:

Date:_____ Time:_____

Is the feeling good or bad?

How strong is the feeling? (Circle a number)

1 2 3 4 5 6 7 8 9 10

How would you categorize this feeling?

- ○ Difference between the gender I feel I am and the sex I was assigned at birth
- ○ Wanting to remove or change my body parts
- ○ Wanting to have the body parts of another gender
- ○ Wanting to be a different gender than the sex assigned at birth
- ○ Wanting to be treated as a different gender
- ○ Feeling or reacting that is typical for a different gender

Did the feeling have a negative impact? If so, how did it impact you?

- ○ On my emotional health
- ○ On my friends, family, or social life
- ○ On my work or education
- ○ On my self-care (diet, sleep, hygiene, exercise)
- ○ No negative impact

Write out your thoughts:

Date:_____ Time:_____

Is the feeling good or bad?

How strong is the feeling? (Circle a number)

1 2 3 4 5 6 7 8 9 10

How would you categorize this feeling?
- ○ Difference between the gender I feel I am and the sex I was assigned at birth
- ○ Wanting to remove or change my body parts
- ○ Wanting to have the body parts of another gender
- ○ Wanting to be a different gender than the sex assigned at birth
- ○ Wanting to be treated as a different gender
- ○ Feeling or reacting that is typical for a different gender

Did the feeling have a negative impact? If so, how did it impact you?
- ○ On my emotional health
- ○ On my friends, family, or social life
- ○ On my work or education
- ○ On my self-care (diet, sleep, hygiene, exercise)
- ○ No negative impact

Write out your thoughts:

Date:_____ Time:_____

Is the feeling good or bad?

How strong is the feeling? (Circle a number)

1   2   3   4   5   6   7   8   9   10

How would you categorize this feeling?

- ○ Difference between the gender I feel I am and the sex I was assigned at birth
- ○ Wanting to remove or change my body parts
- ○ Wanting to have the body parts of another gender
- ○ Wanting to be a different gender than the sex assigned at birth
- ○ Wanting to be treated as a different gender
- ○ Feeling or reacting that is typical for a different gender

Did the feeling have a negative impact? If so, how did it impact you?

- ○ On my emotional health
- ○ On my friends, family, or social life
- ○ On my work or education
- ○ On my self-care (diet, sleep, hygiene, exercise)
- ○ No negative impact

Write out your thoughts:

Date:_____   **Time:**_____

Is the feeling good or bad?

How strong is the feeling? (Circle a number)

1   2   3   4   5   6   7   8   9   10

How would you categorize this feeling?

- Difference between the gender I feel I am and the sex I was assigned at birth
- Wanting to remove or change my body parts
- Wanting to have the body parts of another gender
- Wanting to be a different gender than the sex assigned at birth
- Wanting to be treated as a different gender
- Feeling or reacting that is typical for a different gender

Did the feeling have a negative impact? If so, how did it impact you?

- On my emotional health
- On my friends, family, or social life
- On my work or education
- On my self-care (diet, sleep, hygiene, exercise)
- No negative impact

Write out your thoughts:

Date:_____ Time:_____

Is the feeling good or bad?

How strong is the feeling? (Circle a number)

1   2   3   4   5   6   7   8   9   10

How would you categorize this feeling?

- ○ Difference between the gender I feel I am and the sex I was assigned at birth
- ○ Wanting to remove or change my body parts
- ○ Wanting to have the body parts of another gender
- ○ Wanting to be a different gender than the sex assigned at birth
- ○ Wanting to be treated as a different gender
- ○ Feeling or reacting that is typical for a different gender

Did the feeling have a negative impact? If so, how did it impact you?

- ○ On my emotional health
- ○ On my friends, family, or social life
- ○ On my work or education
- ○ On my self-care (diet, sleep, hygiene, exercise)
- ○ No negative impact

Write out your thoughts:

Date:_____ Time:_____

Is the feeling good or bad?

How strong is the feeling? (Circle a number)

1   2   3   4   5   6   7   8   9   10

How would you categorize this feeling?
- Difference between the gender I feel I am and the sex I was assigned at birth
- Wanting to remove or change my body parts
- Wanting to have the body parts of another gender
- Wanting to be a different gender than the sex assigned at birth
- Wanting to be treated as a different gender
- Feeling or reacting that is typical for a different gender

Did the feeling have a negative impact? If so, how did it impact you?
- On my emotional health
- On my friends, family, or social life
- On my work or education
- On my self-care (diet, sleep, hygiene, exercise)
- No negative impact

Write out your thoughts:

Date:_____ Time:_____

Is the feeling good or bad?

How strong is the feeling? (Circle a number)

1   2   3   4   5   6   7   8   9   10

How would you categorize this feeling?
- Difference between the gender I feel I am and the sex I was assigned at birth
- Wanting to remove or change my body parts
- Wanting to have the body parts of another gender
- Wanting to be a different gender than the sex assigned at birth
- Wanting to be treated as a different gender
- Feeling or reacting that is typical for a different gender

Did the feeling have a negative impact? If so, how did it impact you?
- On my emotional health
- On my friends, family, or social life
- On my work or education
- On my self-care (diet, sleep, hygiene, exercise)
- No negative impact

Write out your thoughts:

Date:_____ Time:_____

Is the feeling good or bad?

How strong is the feeling? (Circle a number)

1   2   3   4   5   6   7   8   9   10

How would you categorize this feeling?
- Difference between the gender I feel I am and the sex I was assigned at birth
- Wanting to remove or change my body parts
- Wanting to have the body parts of another gender
- Wanting to be a different gender than the sex assigned at birth
- Wanting to be treated as a different gender
- Feeling or reacting that is typical for a different gender

Did the feeling have a negative impact? If so, how did it impact you?
- On my emotional health
- On my friends, family, or social life
- On my work or education
- On my self-care (diet, sleep, hygiene, exercise)
- No negative impact

Write out your thoughts:

Date:_____   Time:_____

Is the feeling good or bad?

How strong is the feeling? (Circle a number)

1   2   3   4   5   6   7   8   9   10

How would you categorize this feeling?
- ○ Difference between the gender I feel I am and the sex I was assigned at birth
- ○ Wanting to remove or change my body parts
- ○ Wanting to have the body parts of another gender
- ○ Wanting to be a different gender than the sex assigned at birth
- ○ Wanting to be treated as a different gender
- ○ Feeling or reacting that is typical for a different gender

Did the feeling have a negative impact? If so, how did it impact you?
- ○ On my emotional health
- ○ On my friends, family, or social life
- ○ On my work or education
- ○ On my self-care (diet, sleep, hygiene, exercise)
- ○ No negative impact

Write out your thoughts:

Date:_____ Time:_____

Is the feeling good or bad?

How strong is the feeling? (Circle a number)

1   2   3   4   5   6   7   8   9   10

How would you categorize this feeling?
- Difference between the gender I feel I am and the sex I was assigned at birth
- Wanting to remove or change my body parts
- Wanting to have the body parts of another gender
- Wanting to be a different gender than the sex assigned at birth
- Wanting to be treated as a different gender
- Feeling or reacting that is typical for a different gender

Did the feeling have a negative impact? If so, how did it impact you?
- On my emotional health
- On my friends, family, or social life
- On my work or education
- On my self-care (diet, sleep, hygiene, exercise)
- No negative impact

Write out your thoughts:

Date:_____ Time:_____

Is the feeling good or bad?

How strong is the feeling? (Circle a number)

1   2   3   4   5   6   7   8   9   10

How would you categorize this feeling?
- Difference between the gender I feel I am and the sex I was assigned at birth
- Wanting to remove or change my body parts
- Wanting to have the body parts of another gender
- Wanting to be a different gender than the sex assigned at birth
- Wanting to be treated as a different gender
- Feeling or reacting that is typical for a different gender

Did the feeling have a negative impact? If so, how did it impact you?
- On my emotional health
- On my friends, family, or social life
- On my work or education
- On my self-care (diet, sleep, hygiene, exercise)
- No negative impact

Write out your thoughts:

Date:_____ Time:_____

Is the feeling good or bad?

How strong is the feeling? (Circle a number)

1 2 3 4 5 6 7 8 9 10

How would you categorize this feeling?
- ○ Difference between the gender I feel I am and the sex I was assigned at birth
- ○ Wanting to remove or change my body parts
- ○ Wanting to have the body parts of another gender
- ○ Wanting to be a different gender than the sex assigned at birth
- ○ Wanting to be treated as a different gender
- ○ Feeling or reacting that is typical for a different gender

Did the feeling have a negative impact? If so, how did it impact you?
- ○ On my emotional health
- ○ On my friends, family, or social life
- ○ On my work or education
- ○ On my self-care (diet, sleep, hygiene, exercise)
- ○ No negative impact

Write out your thoughts:

Date:_____ Time:_____

Is the feeling good or bad?

How strong is the feeling? (Circle a number)

1 2 3 4 5 6 7 8 9 10

How would you categorize this feeling?
- ○ Difference between the gender I feel I am and the sex I was assigned at birth
- ○ Wanting to remove or change my body parts
- ○ Wanting to have the body parts of another gender
- ○ Wanting to be a different gender than the sex assigned at birth
- ○ Wanting to be treated as a different gender
- ○ Feeling or reacting that is typical for a different gender

Did the feeling have a negative impact? If so, how did it impact you?
- ○ On my emotional health
- ○ On my friends, family, or social life
- ○ On my work or education
- ○ On my self-care (diet, sleep, hygiene, exercise)
- ○ No negative impact

Write out your thoughts:

Date:_____ **Time:**_____

Is the feeling good or bad?

How strong is the feeling? (Circle a number)

1 2 3 4 5 6 7 8 9 10

How would you categorize this feeling?
- Difference between the gender I feel I am and the sex I was assigned at birth
- Wanting to remove or change my body parts
- Wanting to have the body parts of another gender
- Wanting to be a different gender than the sex assigned at birth
- Wanting to be treated as a different gender
- Feeling or reacting that is typical for a different gender

Did the feeling have a negative impact? If so, how did it impact you?
- On my emotional health
- On my friends, family, or social life
- On my work or education
- On my self-care (diet, sleep, hygiene, exercise)
- No negative impact

Write out your thoughts:

Date:_____ **Time:**_____

Is the feeling good or bad?

How strong is the feeling? (Circle a number)
1 2 3 4 5 6 7 8 9 10

How would you categorize this feeling?
- Difference between the gender I feel I am and the sex I was assigned at birth
- Wanting to remove or change my body parts
- Wanting to have the body parts of another gender
- Wanting to be a different gender than the sex assigned at birth
- Wanting to be treated as a different gender
- Feeling or reacting that is typical for a different gender

Did the feeling have a negative impact? If so, how did it impact you?
- On my emotional health
- On my friends, family, or social life
- On my work or education
- On my self-care (diet, sleep, hygiene, exercise)
- No negative impact

Write out your thoughts:

Date:_____ Time:_____

Is the feeling good or bad?

How strong is the feeling? (Circle a number)

1 2 3 4 5 6 7 8 9 10

How would you categorize this feeling?
- ○ Difference between the gender I feel I am and the sex I was assigned at birth
- ○ Wanting to remove or change my body parts
- ○ Wanting to have the body parts of another gender
- ○ Wanting to be a different gender than the sex assigned at birth
- ○ Wanting to be treated as a different gender
- ○ Feeling or reacting that is typical for a different gender

Did the feeling have a negative impact? If so, how did it impact you?
- ○ On my emotional health
- ○ On my friends, family, or social life
- ○ On my work or education
- ○ On my self-care (diet, sleep, hygiene, exercise)
- ○ No negative impact

Write out your thoughts:

Date:_____ Time:_____

Is the feeling good or bad?

How strong is the feeling? (Circle a number)

1   2   3   4   5   6   7   8   9   10

How would you categorize this feeling?
- Difference between the gender I feel I am and the sex I was assigned at birth
- Wanting to remove or change my body parts
- Wanting to have the body parts of another gender
- Wanting to be a different gender than the sex assigned at birth
- Wanting to be treated as a different gender
- Feeling or reacting that is typical for a different gender

Did the feeling have a negative impact? If so, how did it impact you?
- On my emotional health
- On my friends, family, or social life
- On my work or education
- On my self-care (diet, sleep, hygiene, exercise)
- No negative impact

Write out your thoughts:

Date:_____ Time:_____

Is the feeling good or bad?

How strong is the feeling? (Circle a number)

1 2 3 4 5 6 7 8 9 10

How would you categorize this feeling?
- Difference between the gender I feel I am and the sex I was assigned at birth
- Wanting to remove or change my body parts
- Wanting to have the body parts of another gender
- Wanting to be a different gender than the sex assigned at birth
- Wanting to be treated as a different gender
- Feeling or reacting that is typical for a different gender

Did the feeling have a negative impact? If so, how did it impact you?
- On my emotional health
- On my friends, family, or social life
- On my work or education
- On my self-care (diet, sleep, hygiene, exercise)
- No negative impact

Write out your thoughts:

Date:_____   **Time:**_____

Is the feeling good or bad?

How strong is the feeling? (Circle a number)

1   2   3   4   5   6   7   8   9   10

How would you categorize this feeling?
- Difference between the gender I feel I am and the sex I was assigned at birth
- Wanting to remove or change my body parts
- Wanting to have the body parts of another gender
- Wanting to be a different gender than the sex assigned at birth
- Wanting to be treated as a different gender
- Feeling or reacting that is typical for a different gender

Did the feeling have a negative impact? If so, how did it impact you?
- On my emotional health
- On my friends, family, or social life
- On my work or education
- On my self-care (diet, sleep, hygiene, exercise)
- No negative impact

Write out your thoughts:

Date:_____ Time:_____

Is the feeling good or bad?

How strong is the feeling? (Circle a number)

1 2 3 4 5 6 7 8 9 10

How would you categorize this feeling?
- ○ Difference between the gender I feel I am and the sex I was assigned at birth
- ○ Wanting to remove or change my body parts
- ○ Wanting to have the body parts of another gender
- ○ Wanting to be a different gender than the sex assigned at birth
- ○ Wanting to be treated as a different gender
- ○ Feeling or reacting that is typical for a different gender

Did the feeling have a negative impact? If so, how did it impact you?
- ○ On my emotional health
- ○ On my friends, family, or social life
- ○ On my work or education
- ○ On my self-care (diet, sleep, hygiene, exercise)
- ○ No negative impact

Write out your thoughts:

Date:_____ Time:_____

Is the feeling good or bad?

How strong is the feeling? (Circle a number)

1   2   3   4   5   6   7   8   9   10

How would you categorize this feeling?
- ○ Difference between the gender I feel I am and the sex I was assigned at birth
- ○ Wanting to remove or change my body parts
- ○ Wanting to have the body parts of another gender
- ○ Wanting to be a different gender than the sex assigned at birth
- ○ Wanting to be treated as a different gender
- ○ Feeling or reacting that is typical for a different gender

Did the feeling have a negative impact? If so, how did it impact you?
- ○ On my emotional health
- ○ On my friends, family, or social life
- ○ On my work or education
- ○ On my self-care (diet, sleep, hygiene, exercise)
- ○ No negative impact

Write out your thoughts:

Date: _____   **Time:** _____

Is the feeling good or bad?

How strong is the feeling? (Circle a number)

1   2   3   4   5   6   7   8   9   10

How would you categorize this feeling?
- ○ Difference between the gender I feel I am and the sex I was assigned at birth
- ○ Wanting to remove or change my body parts
- ○ Wanting to have the body parts of another gender
- ○ Wanting to be a different gender than the sex assigned at birth
- ○ Wanting to be treated as a different gender
- ○ Feeling or reacting that is typical for a different gender

Did the feeling have a negative impact? If so, how did it impact you?
- ○ On my emotional health
- ○ On my friends, family, or social life
- ○ On my work or education
- ○ On my self-care (diet, sleep, hygiene, exercise)
- ○ No negative impact

Write out your thoughts:

Date:_____ **Time:**_____

Is the feeling good or bad?

How strong is the feeling? (Circle a number)

1   2   3   4   5   6   7   8   9   10

How would you categorize this feeling?
- Difference between the gender I feel I am and the sex I was assigned at birth
- Wanting to remove or change my body parts
- Wanting to have the body parts of another gender
- Wanting to be a different gender than the sex assigned at birth
- Wanting to be treated as a different gender
- Feeling or reacting that is typical for a different gender

Did the feeling have a negative impact? If so, how did it impact you?
- On my emotional health
- On my friends, family, or social life
- On my work or education
- On my self-care (diet, sleep, hygiene, exercise)
- No negative impact

Write out your thoughts:

Made in the USA
Middletown, DE
09 September 2023